THE GREAT CONN

A True-Life American Hero

BY

M J SCHULTZ

AND

MUHAMMAD JEHANGIR KHAN

The Great Conn: A True-Life Story

Copyright © 2025 by MJ Schultz and Muhammad Jehangir Khan

All rights reserved. No part of this book may be reproduced, distributed, or transmitted in any form or by any means, including photocopying, recording, or other electronic or mechanical methods, without the prior written permission of the publisher, except in the case of brief quotations embodied in reviews, critical articles, or educational use.

This is a work of narrative nonfiction. While based on real events and historical figures, certain dialogue and scenes have been dramatized for literary effect.

CONTENTS

I have witnessed greatness. I have seen legends ascend, fall, and rise again. I have watched Muhammad Ali at his fiercest, both inside and outside the ring. I know what it means to stand toe-to-toe with history. When I think of fairness, integrity, and moral strength, one name stands out: Mark Conn.

Mark was more than a referee. He was calm amid chaos, the one who kept titans honest. He knew when to release them and when to rein them in. He managed more than fights. He stewarded humanity.

I met Mark during Ali's 1970s return. His precision in the ring impressed me, but even more so, the peace he brought. There was softness beneath his strength and a smile behind his command. Ali respected him. The world did. So, did I.

This book, *The Great Conn*, is more than a biography. It honors a man who stood tall without seeking the spotlight. A man who fought wars, raised a family, danced with humor, and loved deeply. His story reminds us: you do not have to throw punches to be a true fighter.

To every young reader, let this story teach you: about grace, grit, and showing up, even when the lights dim. Mark Conn did. That's why he'll never be forgotten.

Dr. Khalilah Camacho Ali (Mama Ali)
Past wife of Muhammad Ali
Author, public speaker, and humanitarian

Mama Ali

Before the lights of Madison Square Garden. Before the roar of thousands or the glint of title belts. Before the 21-gun salute and the tributes. Before Ali, before Foreman, before LaMotta ever met his match.

There was a boy with scuffed shoes and a sharp wit, running down a Brooklyn block with a red glove on his hand and the world in his heart.

Mark Conn wasn't born into fame. He was born into a fight, the kind with bills on the table and dreams too big for the room. His father had fists like bricks and a voice like thunder. His mother had quiet eyes that saw everything. The Conn home was filled with laughter and shouting and hard-earned love.

And in the middle of it, Mark learned his first lesson: *how to hold space in a storm.*

He would learn to box in the shadows of real champions. He'd fly planes in a war halfway across the globe. He'd raise kids with bedtime jokes and bridge tournaments. He'd stand between the most powerful men in the world and say one word that held it all together: *"Break."*

This is not the story of a perfect man. It's the story of a man who kept showing up, with honor, with humor, with heart.

This is *The Great Conn.*

And it all began with one pair of red gloves.

Signed photograph of Muhammad Ali and his wife, Dr. Khalilah Ali Camacho, gifted to the author. A personal glimpse into the warmth behind the legend.

Chapter 1

Red Gloves in Brooklyn (1930)

The air was heavy with the smell of coal smoke and boiled cabbage that drifted through the narrow hallways of the apartment building on Hart Street in Brooklyn. Fourteen-year-old Mark Conn sat on the cold front stoop, knees pulled tight to his chest, watching the neighborhood boys toss a crumpled newspaper back and forth. It was early autumn, 1930, and the leaves that gathered at the curb seemed just as restless as the city boys who kicked at them.

Mark's worn boots tapped lightly on the step. He didn't have much. Most days were spent running errands for his mother or dodging the slaps of street fights he didn't start but rarely backed down from. He didn't know it then, but a single knock on the door that afternoon would shift the axis of his entire life.

"Markie!" came a voice from upstairs.

It was Alex. Twenty-three, broad-shouldered, hair slicked back with pomade, and always wearing that worn leather jacket like he had just stepped out of a moving picture. Alex was the kind of man who carried himself with a confidence that made boys watch and old men nod. He had returned about a year ago, and when he wasn't working the docks, he trained at the gym near Fulton Street.

Mark jumped up. "Hey, Alex."

Alex grinned, one hand behind his back. "Got something for you, kid."

Mark's eyes narrowed with curiosity. "What is it?"

From behind his back, Alex produced a pair of boxing gloves. Not just any gloves, red leather, scuffed at the knuckles, but solid, the kind that smelled like sweat and liniment. They looked massive in Alex's hands, but somehow felt just right when he handed them over.

"They were mine," Alex said. "Wore 'em through two seasons at St. Mary's Gym. Thought it was time they found new fists."

Mark turned them over in his hands as though he'd just been given the keys to something sacred. The gloves were soft but firm, worn but not weak. His heart thudded in his chest.

"I can't pay you for these," he whispered.

"They're not for sale," Alex said with a wink. "They're for fighting the right way. You've got something in you, Mark. I've seen it. You don't back down. That's a start."

Mark blinked, unsure how to respond. No one had ever said something like that to him. His world had been all noise, shouting, scraping, dodging. But this moment was still. Weighty.

Alex clapped a hand on Mark's shoulder. "Come by the gym tomorrow. I'll show you the ropes. Literally."

Mark nodded slowly, gripping the gloves close to his chest. "I will. I promise."

The door creaked behind them as Mark's mother peeked out, wiping her hands on a flour-dusted apron. Her eyes moved from Alex to the gloves to her son.

"What's this?"

"He's training now," Alex said before Mark could answer. "St. Mary's. We'll keep him out of trouble."

Her face tightened for a moment, worry and weariness etched into every line, but she gave a soft nod. "Just don't let him come home with a busted nose."

Alex smiled. "No promises."

That night, Mark didn't sleep much. He lay on the thin mattress in the corner of their one-bedroom flat, the red gloves next to his pillow. His fingers ached to try them on again. Something had shifted inside him, a hunger he hadn't known was waiting. He wasn't just a boy from Hart Street anymore.

He was a boy with gloves. A boy with a path.

And he would never forget who gave him that first spark.

The winter of 1930 bit hard in New York, but Mark Conn never let the cold bite deeper than his will. With the red gloves in his knapsack and Alex's words still echoing in his head, Mark made his way through the maze of Brooklyn and into Queens. He trained wherever space allowed, handball courts with cracked concrete walls, sandlots frozen stiff, school basements that smelled of dust and sweat. There was no comfort in these places, only work.

He rose before the sun, laced his shoes with string where the laces had split, and jogged down the frozen sidewalks while others still slept. His breath made steam in the air, and the gloves swung rhythmically from his side like a heartbeat.

Alex met him twice a week when he could. On Sundays, they caught the train to a church gym that let neighborhood kids spar for free, provided they mopped the floors afterward. On weekdays, Mark trained alone. His favorite spot was a worn handball court behind an old school in Queens. The wall was pockmarked and uneven, but it didn't matter. He'd wrap a towel around a brick, tie it to a rope, and swing it from the court fence like a makeshift punching bag.

Jab. Step. Jab-jab. Hook. Duck.

He repeated the sequence until his arms burned. He had no trainer shouting combinations, no timer buzzing between rounds. Just instinct, repetition, and drive.

Kids watched from the chain-link fence sometimes. A few laughed, some pointed. One boy yelled, "Hey, Red Gloves!" and the name stuck. Mark didn't mind. It gave him a kind of identity; a badge earned in silence.

"Red Gloves don't quit," he'd mutter to himself.

He shadowboxed by storefront windows to correct his form, studied how his hips turned when he pivoted, how his left shoulder rose to shield his jaw. His movements were tight, self-taught, but surprisingly disciplined. He learned the rhythm of his own body before he ever heard the bell of a real ring.

Money was thin. The Depression tightened its grip on everyone. At home, dinner might be stale bread and boiled onions. Sometimes nothing. But Mark never missed a day of training. He ran deliveries for the grocer. Shined shoes on corners. Anything to scrape together a few nickels to buy handwraps or replace the threadbare socks that gave him blisters inside his shoes.

One Saturday, Alex found him out behind the courts, sweat freezing at the edge of his hairline.

"You're overtraining," Alex warned, tossing him a towel.

Mark shook his head. "I'm behind."

"Behind who?"

"Everyone."

Alex looked him over, scrawny but wiry, fists taped with scraps of torn shirt, nose slightly crooked from a street fight that week. But his eyes? Focused. Sharp.

"You're ahead," Alex said. "You're ahead because you care more than they do. Most of those kids don't know what hunger feels like. You do. That's your edge."

Mark said nothing. He just nodded, turned back to the wall, and kept going.

By spring, he had outgrown the brick on a rope. He found an old mattress and tied it to the fence. The gift was better. More lifelike. When he punched it, he imagined an opponent, fast, strong, relentless.

Sometimes it was the boy who used to push him around in school. Sometimes it was the feeling of being small, unseen, poor.

But more often, it was no one.

It was just Mark and the wall, and the fire that lived in his chest.

One jab at a time, Red Gloves was becoming a fighter.

The bell at St. Mary's Gym rang sharp and cold, bouncing off the cracked tile walls like a summons. It wasn't much to look at, a church basement with two hanging bulbs, worn-out mats, and an old canvas ring patched at the corners, but to Mark Conn, it felt like a cathedral.

Alex stood ringside, arms folded, watching as Mark danced between the ropes in borrowed shoes and his own red gloves. He was sixteen now, leaner than most of the boys but never the smallest in presence. His footwork was tighter, crisper than even some of the regulars. When he moved, it wasn't fancy, but it had purpose, every step building into the next like bricks forming a wall.

"Keep your chin down, Red," Alex called. "Gloves high."

Mark adjusted without breaking rhythm. Sweat dripped down his jaw, but he did not wipe it. His eyes stayed locked on the shadow of an opponent that only he could see.

It had been two years since Alex had handed him the gloves. Two years of relentless practice, calloused knuckles, skipped meals, and split lips. But Mark never complained. He never asked how much longer until he was good enough. He just showed up.

That's what Alex admired most.

Some boys came to the gym looking for a fight. Others came to win. But Mark came to become.

Between rounds, Alex would lean in and whisper corrections, elbow in tighter, jab before the hook, slip left instead of right. Mark absorbed every word. He didn't argue. Didn't shrug. Just nodded once and applied it.

"You notice?" one of the trainers murmured to Alex one evening. "Kid's got something."

"Yeah," Alex replied. "Discipline. Doesn't fade."

Discipline, not talent, was the difference. That was what Alex believed, and Mark proved it. While others missed sessions for dates, parties, or excuses, Mark was always there. Even when his knuckles bled through his wraps, even when his shoes cracked open at the toe. He never asked for new ones.

He earned everything.

They ran drills at the Queens handball courts, did roadwork through backstreets at sunrise, and sparred in empty rings when no one was watching. When Mark lost a round, he didn't sulk; he reviewed it in his mind like a movie reel, breaking down every mistake until it made sense.

One cold evening, after a long session, Alex handed him a worn notebook.

"What's this?" Mark asked, wiping sweat from his neck with the hem of his shirt.

"Your record book," Alex said. "Write down what you did each day. What went wrong? What felt right. Patterns make champions."

Mark opened it to the first page and wrote in pencil: *Three rounds. Missed my right hook. Breathe better next time.*

It wasn't poetry. But it was honest.

Alex smiled.

One day, they stayed late after everyone else had gone. The gym was quiet except for the creak of the ropes and the low hum of the radiator. Alex stepped into the ring with him.

"No rounds. Just rhythm."

They moved in slow motion. Alex jabbed, Mark blocked. Alex feinted, Mark shifted. It was a silent dance, mentor and student, past and future.

When they stopped, Mark was breathing hard, chest rising and falling in a steady rhythm.

"You're starting to feel it," Alex said.

Mark nodded. "I don't think anymore. I just moved."

"That's when you know it's real."

Mark looked at his gloves, the same red ones from two years ago, now darker with age and sweat. "You ever think I could go pro?"

Alex didn't answer right away.

Instead, he put a hand on Mark's shoulder and said, "I think you were born to be more than just a fighter."

Chapter 2

"Champ" is Born (1936)

The arena lights hummed overhead like nervous electricity. It was March 1936, and the crowd at Madison Square Garden buzzed with the pulse of a city that needed something to cheer for. The Great Depression still lingered, but tonight, for a few hours, hope wore gloves and danced under spotlights.

Mark Conn stood in the corner, twenty years old, jaw clenched, eyes locked on the center of the ring. The robe draped over his shoulders was borrowed. The gloves were scuffed. But the fire in his chest was his alone.

Across from him stood Frankie D'Angelo, strong, flashy, undefeated in the tournament so far. Frankie had a following. Mark had grit.

Alex adjusted Mark's mouthpiece and gave a final nod. "He's fast, but you're smarter. You've trained for this since you were fourteen."

Mark nodded. "I'm ready."

The bell rang.

Round one was chaos. Frankie opened with a storm of jabs, sharp and arrogant. The crowd roared with every connection, but Mark didn't flinch. He moved like water, bending, slipping, letting the punches whistle past.

"Keep your feet! Watch the shoulder drop!" Alex shouted from the corner.

Midway through the round, Mark caught Frankie with a left hook. Clean. The crowd gasped.

Round two was tighter. Mark began to study the rhythm, how Frankie circled left after his jab, how he dropped his right hand on the feint. By the third round, Mark's timing was surgical. He wasn't fighting just a man; he was solving a puzzle in motion.

"Conn lands another combination!" the announcer called.

The judges leaned forward. The crowd sensed the shift.

In the fourth, Frankie swung wide. Mark ducked low, stepped in, and drove a right hand into the ribs that sent his opponent staggering. The bell ended the round, but the momentum had turned.

Alex said nothing between rounds. Just handed him water and nodded. Mark didn't need words anymore. He was in a place beyond thought, where training met instinct.

Final round.

Frankie came out desperate. Wild. Mark stayed calm, crisp. He slipped to the right, jabbed twice, pivoted left, and drove a shot into Frankie's chin that sent the bigger fighter crashing to the canvas.

The referee's count echoed through the Garden.

"One! Two! Three…"

Frankie rose, barely, but the decision was clear.

When the bell rang, Mark didn't raise his hands. He just stood still, breathing, gloves lowered, chest rising and falling in quiet rhythm. He had done it.

The ring announcer stepped forward.

"Ladies and gentlemen, the winner of the 1936 New York Golden Gloves Lightweight Division, Mark Conn!"

The crowd erupted.

Alex wrapped him in a hug. "You did it, Champ."

The word stuck.

That night, Mark's name ran in the papers. "Conn Shocks Favorite at Garden," read one. Another called him "A Working-Class Miracle in Red Gloves." But it was the nickname that spread fastest.

Kids outside the gym started calling him "Champ" before they even knew his first name.

Mark didn't smile for the camera. He was never one for showboating. But deep inside, something shifted. Not pride. Not fame. Just a quiet confirmation.

He belonged.

Outside the Garden, he walked home in the cold, robe over his shoulder, trophy tucked under his arm. The city lights blurred in the mist, but one thing was clear.

A new name had been born that night.

Champ.

The gym smelled like sweat, old rope, and winter steam rising from heavy coats. It was a few weeks after his Golden Gloves victory, and the city still whispered Mark Conn's name. But Mark didn't care about the headlines. He was back at St. Mary's, back in the ring, back where the noise outside couldn't reach him.

Then came the letter.

Alex handed it to him with a grin that broke through his usual stone face.

"Open it, Champ."

Mark wiped his hands on his towel and peeled it open. The letterhead read *Metropolitan Amateur Boxing Association.* The rest he read twice.

He had been chosen for the Yale Rubin Trophy, an honor given to the top amateur boxer in New York.

He blinked. "I didn't even know I was in the running."

"You didn't have to," Alex said. "You earned it."

The ceremony was held in a modest banquet hall downtown. The kind of place with white tablecloths and folding chairs that creaked when you sat. Mark wore a secondhand suit. Alex wore the same brown coat he'd always had.

Sportswriters, trainers, and former champions filled the room. Some clinked glasses, others told stories of fights from a decade ago. When Mark entered, conversations paused. Heads turned. The kid who beat Frankie D'Angelo was no longer just a street fighter with a good chin; he was a name.

They called him to the front after a long list of speeches. The emcee, an old columnist with a heavy voice, tapped the microphone.

"This year's Yale Rubin Trophy goes to a young man who reminds us why this sport still matters. No sponsors. No pedigree. Just grit, heart, and discipline. Ladies and gentlemen, Mark Conn."

Applause rolled through the room. Mark stood slowly, unsure how to carry himself in a room full of praise.

He walked to the stage, accepted the wooden plaque with the brass engraving, and shook the man's hand. Flashes from press cameras dotted the moment, but Mark barely noticed.

He stepped to the microphone.

"Thank you," he said simply. "This means a lot. I don't fight for trophies, but I'll carry this one with pride. For my neighborhood. For Alex. And for every kid who thinks he doesn't have a shot."

That was it.

He stepped down, applause trailing him.

Later that night, at a diner on Flatbush, he and Alex sat in a booth, the trophy between them.

"You didn't flinch up there," Alex said.

Mark stirred his coffee. "I'd rather take a punch than make a speech."

Alex laughed. "Well, you're getting better at both."

Mark looked at the plaque. "Yale Rubin. He was a writer, right?"

"Yeah. Covered boxing for forty years. Wrote like a poet, fought like a brawler when he was young."

Mark nodded. "Feels strange, getting his name."

"It's not about the name," Alex said. "It's what people believe when they hear yours."

The trophy didn't change Mark. The next morning, he was back at the gym by seven. Jumping rope. Working the heavy bag. Writing notes in his little notebook. His fame didn't make him louder. It made him quieter. Focused. Aware that more eyes meant more responsibility.

But in the corners of the gym, whispers had started.

"He's gonna go all the way."

"Pro scouts are coming next week."

"Kids got the Rubin Trophy, he's real now."

Mark didn't answer the whispers. He just laced up his gloves and stepped into the ring.

The shine of the brass plaque faded with time. But the weight of it never left his shoulders.

Not because it made him important.

Because it reminded him of why he started.

The morning sky over Brooklyn was slate grey, the kind that made the city feel heavier. It was late 1936, and the buzz of the world beyond the boroughs had begun to seep into even the thickest gym walls. Radios murmured headlines about Europe, strange names, and distant fears. Men read newspapers with furrowed brows, their coffee growing cold beside them.

Mark Conn stood on the rooftop of the tenement, gloves slung over his shoulder, gazing out as a low-flying aircraft hummed across the clouds. It moved with the grace of something untouchable, something freer than the fists and footwork that had defined his world for the past six years.

Alex found him there, arms crossed, watching the sky.

"You're quiet," he said.

Mark didn't turn. "That's a Waco biplane. Same model I saw last week flying out of Roosevelt Field."

Alex raised an eyebrow. "You been studying planes now?"

"Yeah," Mark replied. "I go by the airstrip sometimes. Watch 'em take off. Something about it... feels right."

Alex stood beside him in silence.

Mark turned to face him. "I think I want to learn. How to fly, I mean."

Alex didn't answer right away. He reached into his coat, lit a cigarette, and exhaled slowly. "Boxing and flying are two different kinds of sky, kid."

"I know," Mark said. "But there's something calling me to it. I can feel it. Like when I first put on those gloves."

Alex gave a short laugh. "You think you'll trade the ring for the clouds?"

Mark smiled faintly. "Maybe not trade. Just... add to it."

The war in Europe was still whispered about in New York, but the whispers were growing louder. Posters had begun to appear near shipyards and recruitment offices. Words like "patriotism" and "readiness" floated through neighborhoods like storm warnings. The world was shifting, and Mark, who had always kept his eyes focused inside the ropes, was beginning to look outward.

He started reading at night, manuals, maps, and journals by American pilots. The same discipline that made him a champion in the ring began shaping a new kind of dream. He memorized plane models, studied weather patterns, and wrote notes in a small spiral notebook he kept hidden under his mattress.

He didn't speak about it much. Just once, to his mother, while helping her fix a broken radio.

"Ma," he said gently, "you ever think of going somewhere far away?"

She looked at him over her glasses. "I thought of it every day after your father died."

Mark smiled. "I think I want to fly. For real."

She nodded slowly. "Then fly. Just promise me you'll come back."

Word spread, as it always did. Some in the neighborhood scoffed. "Conn's heads in the clouds," they said. Others nodded with respect. "Takes guts to dream again after winning so much."

But Mark didn't talk about dreams. He kept training, kept fighting, but in the quiet spaces, in between matches, in the still moments before dawn, his mind drifted skyward.

At the gym, Alex watched him more closely now. He noticed how Mark's movements had changed. There was more lightness, more calculation. As if he wasn't just fighting opponents, but gravity itself.

"You sure about this?" Alex asked one night after training.

"I've never been surer," Mark said.

Alex looked at him for a long time.

"Then when the time comes," he said, "you fly. But promise me one thing."

"What's that?"

"Don't stop fighting."

Mark nodded. "I won't. Just trading canvas for clouds."

And so, quietly, a new dream took shape. Not born in applause or spotlight, but in the silent pull of the sky. Where fists once led him to victory, wings now whispered of purpose.

The Champ was still here.

But the Pilot had begun to rise.

The dusty airfield baked under the midday sun, far from the skyline of Brooklyn and the roar of Madison Square Garden. This was China, 1941. A different world, a different war. And Mark Conn, once the pride of New York's boxing rings, now stood in the tan uniform of the American Volunteer Group, the legendary Flying Tigers.

It had been a long road from red gloves to cockpit gauges.

Back home, when Mark first heard the name General Claire Chennault, he had scribbled it in the corner of his notebook. A commander with a vision, fast planes, sharp instincts, and small forces against overwhelming odds. It sounded like boxing in the sky.

By early 1941, the whispers of war had grown into a full-throated roar. Roosevelt's America teetered on the edge of involvement. But the fight had already started elsewhere. China was burning, and the Japanese advance was relentless. Volunteers were needed, men with guts, skills, and a cause

worth more than medals.

Mark signed on.

He left behind the familiar rhythm of the bag and the bell, traded for the roar of the Curtiss P-40 Warhawk engine

and the sharp wind of high-altitude combat.

Members of the American Volunteer Group flew Curtiss P-40 planes, pictured. By performing certain maneuvers, they were able to exploit some weaknesses in the Japanese aircraft. **Three Lions/Getty Images**

Yet not everything from his past was left behind. In a camp just outside Kunming, he was known not just as a pilot, but as 'The Champ,' unofficial boxing instructor and Athletic Director of the Flying Tigers.

Pilots from the American Volunteer Group sit in front of a P-40 airplane in Kunming, China, on March 27, 1942. The group was notable for its unusual mission: Its members were mercenaries hired by China to fight against Japan.

Chennault, gruff and exacting, had learned of Mark's Golden Gloves record during recruitment. He saw more than just a boxer; he saw morale. Discipline. Toughness. Within weeks, Mark had become the unofficial boxing instructor of the Flying Tigers.

"Conn!" someone shouted across the field one afternoon, as Mark ran drills beside a grounded Warhawk.

It was Lieutenant Harmon, winded and bruised, holding his ribs.

"Next time, Champ, remind me not to jab with my chin."

Mark laughed, offering a hand. "Keep your hands up, Lieutenant. The sky ain't the only place you'll get hit."

Word had spread quickly. Between patrols and mission briefings, the camp's makeshift ring became a second battlefield. Mark taught fundamentals, footwork, combinations, and breathing under pressure. Pilots learned to move smarter, think faster. The same instincts that won fights could save lives in the cockpit.

But boxing wasn't a distraction; it was preparation. Combat flying was its own kind of bout. Enemies came fast, from every direction. There was no bell, no second round. You won or you didn't come back.

Mark adjusted to the rhythm of aerial life. Flight checks at dawn. Patrol runs above rice paddies and mountain ranges. Dogfights that spun the world upside down. The sound of gunfire replaced cheers. The sky became both opponent and arena.

In the evenings, men gathered to watch him shadowbox beside the barracks, his silhouette dancing against the setting sun.

"You ever miss the ring?" one pilot asked him once.

Mark paused. "Sometimes. But up there," he pointed to the sky, now streaked with clouds, "that's where the real fight is."

Though death loomed over every mission, Mark carried himself with calm. Not arrogance, discipline. The kind born on sandlots and Queens handball courts. He had learned long ago how to breathe through chaos, how to wait for an opening, how to fight with purpose.

Claire Lee Commander Chennault watched from a distance, rarely speaking praise aloud. But in the mess tent one evening, he muttered to a staff officer, "That Conn? He brings fight to the ground and the sky. Damn glad he's on our side."

So, from Army recruit to Flying Tiger, Mark Conn carved a new chapter, not as a man chasing glory, but as one answering the call.

And though the gloves were lighter now, the mission was heavier than ever.

December 20, 1941. The date carved itself into Mark Conn's mind like the scar of a first loss in the ring. Only this wasn't Madison Square Garden. This was the sky above Rangoon, and this time, the consequences were measured not in bruises, but in blood and burning steel. The tension of patrols gave way to the gravity of an aerial battle.

The briefing had been short. Japanese bombers were inbound, fast, loaded, and guarded by Zeros. The mission was simple: intercept and protect the Burma Road. If they failed, Rangoon would be crippled.

Mark climbed into his Curtiss P-40 Warhawk, the Tiger's teeth painted wide across the nose. Sweat pooled beneath his helmet. He adjusted the oxygen mask, fingers trembling slightly, unlike the steady hands he once used to

wrap leather gloves.

"Conn, Tiger Four. Cleared for takeoff." The voice crackled in his headset.

He exhaled once, sharp and deep. Just like before a fight.

Then the engine roared to life.

The sky opened above the jungle like an invitation to chaos. They climbed hard, the earth shrinking below. To Mark, it felt like the moments before the opening bell, heart pounding, lungs tight, focus narrowing to a single task: survive.

At 15,000 feet, the enemy appeared.

"Tigers, we've got visuals, ten o'clock high!"

Bristling formation. Bombers, fat with payload, trailed by the silver glints of Zeros darting in protective orbit.

"Split and engage!" came the call.

Mark banked left, rolling into the fray. The first seconds were a blur, tracers, sunbursts of flak, the scream of engines too close for comfort. A Zero streaked past his canopy. He pulled hard on the stick, G-forces crushing his ribs.

He fired.

The .50 caliber roared, vibrating the whole cockpit. The rounds stitched across the sky and bit into metal. One Zero spiraled, smoke trailing like ribbon. It tumbled, disappeared.

Adrenaline surged. The fear didn't vanish; it sharpened.

From the corner of his eye, he saw another Tiger take a hit. A plume. A dive. Gone.

Mark gritted his teeth. "Focus."

He dove after a bomber, closing the distance. Every second was a calculation, angle, speed, wind, ammunition. He could hear Alex's voice in his head: *"Pick your shot. Don't waste energy swinging wild."*

He lined up the tail. Fired.

The bomber shuddered. A burst of flame.

But now the hunters turned. Two Zeros locked onto him.

"Tiger Four, you've got company!" came the warning.

Mark yanked into a dive, cutting low across the clouds. Bullets zipped past, punching through nothing and everything. He banked again, twisted into a roll, and climbed hard.

One of the Zeros is stuck.

Mark weaved, swerved between clouds like a dancer. The tracer fire kissed his wing. Smoke trailed. A hit, but not fatal.

Instinct took over.

He throttled down, jerked into a stall, then kicked the rudder. The Zero overshot.

Mark leveled, aimed, and fired.

It exploded into smoke and silence.

Breathing ragged, he looked around. The airspace was littered, some enemy aircraft falling, some escaping. Tigers regrouping. Others... not responding.

The sky cleared slowly. A voice came through.

"Rangoon is safe for now. Return to base."

Mark didn't answer right away.

He stared ahead, past the glass, through the world. His heart still beat with the rhythm of war drums. His gloves today had been steel and bullets, not leather and tape.

But the principle remained.

Stay calm. Hit clean. Survive.

Back on the ground, there were no cheers. No arms raised. Just nods, heavy steps, and silent gratitude.

Mark climbed from the cockpit, legs shaking.

"First mission?" one mechanic asked.

Mark nodded. "Yeah."

"How was it?"

Mark paused.

"Like stepping into the ring… but the ropes are made of clouds, and there's no bell to save you."

And with that, he walked toward the barracks, alive, but changed.

By the third month in China, Mark Conn had learned that war was never only about the battles in the sky. There was another front, quieter, more enduring, that stretched across dusty villages, along the snake-like curves of the Burma Road, and in the eyes of those who fought without ever firing a shot.

It was here that Mark began to see the true meaning of brotherhood, not just among the pilots of the Flying Tigers, but with the Chinese soldiers and civilians whose resilience seemed carved from the very mountains they defended.

In between missions, Mark found himself stationed near Lashio, where the humidity clung to his skin and the jungle whispered a thousand stories with every rustle of the trees. The American Volunteer Group worked closely with local Nationalist Chinese forces under Chiang Kai-shek's command, and though language remained a barrier, the effort bridged the gap.

Most days were spent repairing aircraft, reviewing maps, and preparing for the next wave of Japanese attacks. But in the slow hours between, Mark found purpose in something different.

He began teaching boxing.

At first, it had been a casual offer. One of the Chinese soldiers, curious about the gloves tucked under Mark's cot, mimicked a punch. Mark smiled, mimicked one back, and the moment grew into a gathering. Within a week, they had cleared a patch of dirt behind the barracks, and each evening after mess, men gathered in a wide circle, barefoot and eager, learning footwork, jabs, and hooks as Mark demonstrated with patience and care.

They laughed together when punches landed too wide. They grunted through clumsy footwork and cheered when someone improved. For the soldiers, it was more than sport; it was strength, discipline, and a kind of dignity that carried over to everything else.

For Mark, it became a ritual. He wasn't just a soldier in the sky anymore; he was a teacher, a friend, a presence that offered something real in a time when so much had been lost.

What struck him most was the silence of heroism in the villagers who lived along the Burma Road. He had seen children with eyes older than their years helping carry ammunition. He had seen women boiling rice in battered pots, sharing it with passing soldiers without asking for anything in return. He had seen old men who had likely survived one war already, now offering shelter to boys barely old enough to shave.

One morning, while scouting a bend of the Burma Road for potential supply routes, Mark rode in a transport truck beside a Chinese captain named Liu. The man spoke decent English and carried himself with the composure of someone who had long since made peace with the idea of dying for his country.

Chinese laborers repair the vital Burma Road, c. 1944.

"They do not fear death here," Liu said, gesturing to the farmers in the fields. "Because every day is already a fight."

Mark watched as a young boy, no older than ten, herded oxen beside an old cart. His arms were thin, his legs scarred, but his gaze was direct, steady in a way that reminded Mark of the way fighters looked before stepping into a ring. Mark swallowed, unsure how to respond.

That evening, he wrapped the boy's fists in cloth and taught him how to punch.

Soon, the boy brought two friends. Then five more.

A silent army was forming, one that didn't fly planes or drop bombs, but learned to stand taller, move smarter, breathe with discipline.

Japanese troops charge Chinese defenses during the Battle of Changsha, 1939 part of Japan's broader offensive in China by 1941.

Mark never gave grand speeches. He didn't speak of America or victory. He only showed them how to move their feet, when to throw, and how to take a hit without losing their balance.

He understood then that bravery wasn't only found in the cockpit. Sometimes, it stood barefoot on packed earth, fists raised not in anger but in the quiet defense of something worth protecting.

Mid-1941, before Pearl Harbor.

Part II: Love, War, and Legacy

Mark Conn stepped off the train at Penn Station in the spring of 1945 with a single duffel bag and a chest full of unspoken memories. The roar of New York felt different now, louder, more crowded, but somehow emptier too. After years of soaring above cities and jungles, the concrete streets of Brooklyn felt almost surreal.

He was home, but he wasn't the same. War had a way of sculpting silence inside a man, and Mark carried that silence behind his eyes.

The first thing he did was head to the old apartment building on 42nd Street, where it had all started, the same place Alex once handed him those red gloves, the same block where he had shadowboxed between parked cars and trained with nothing but hunger. Alex, now 34, had aged like a fighter out of the ring, muscles still firm, but his face marked by the weight of watching too many young men go off to war, including Mark.

"You came back," Alex said simply as they embraced, neither needing to speak of the missions or medals.

That evening, over roast beef and rye in Alex's kitchen, the door swung open and in walked a young woman with dark curls pinned behind her ears, carrying a stack of books and a presence that made Mark sit up straighter. She paused when she saw him, eyebrows raised slightly. Alex looked between them, then gave a knowing chuckle.

"Mark, meet my niece, Betty Siegel. Everyone calls her Boots."

Alex with his 16-year-old niece, Betty Siegel (Boots)

"Boots?" Mark repeated, standing to shake her hand. "Interesting nickname."

"She used to sneak around in her father's combat boots as a kid," Alex offered. "Name stuck."

Boots smiled, and for a second, the war faded from Mark's mind.

Their conversation started over coffee and lingered well into the night. She was twenty-one, sharp, and full of opinions about books, music, and the state of the world. Mark listened more than he spoke, drawn not just to her voice but the way she looked at him, not as a soldier to be admired, but as a man who'd seen too much and was still standing.

Over the weeks that followed, their connection deepened in small, unspoken ways. She would wait for him after he visited the gym or returned from walking the bridge. They strolled through Prospect Park, sat on stoops drinking orange sodas, and spent evenings listening to radio jazz. When she laughed, something settled in Mark's chest, a reminder that life could still be tender.

He told her about Burma, about Liu and the barefoot boys who boxed behind barracks. She told him about college, about wanting to become a teacher, but not liking the idea of staying still. "The world's too big to sit in one classroom forever," she said once, eyes fixed on the horizon.

Their first kiss happened on the Brooklyn Bridge at dusk. The sky was stained orange, the wind tugged gently at her coat, and the city buzzed below like a forgotten song. Mark touched her cheek, and she leaned in as if the war, the years, and all the noise around them had led to this quiet moment.

"I don't scare easily," she whispered.

"Neither do I," Mark replied.

When he walked her home that night, Boots didn't look back at the bridge. She looked at him.

He didn't need red gloves or medals for this fight. Just the courage to stay.

It was a late Sunday afternoon when Boots first discovered the piano in Mark's modest apartment above the tailor shop on Flatbush Avenue. The wooden upright sat tucked in a corner by the window, its varnish dulled by time and its keys slightly uneven, but Boots was drawn to it like a moth to stained glass. Mark had never mentioned music, yet here it was, waiting in silence, like a hidden piece of him.

"You play?" she asked, brushing a fingertip across the ivory.

Mark looked up from the newspaper and smiled. "I used to. Taught myself after school. Used to copy what I heard on the radio. I haven't really touched it since, well, since before everything."

"Play something now," she said, stepping back.

He hesitated, almost shy. But her gaze made the silence warm, not heavy. He sat down, cracked his knuckles once, and placed his fingers on the keys. The first notes were hesitant, searching. Then they found each other. The room filled with a melody, part waltz, part lullaby, with a bluesy undertow. Boots closed her eyes and let the music pull her into a world with no war, no noise, only heartbeat and breath.

"You're not just a boxer," she murmured afterward.

"I never was," he said, almost to himself.

That piano became their quiet ritual. Sunday evenings were reserved for improvised songs and the occasional lesson. Boots would sit beside him, her fingers struggling to keep up, laughing when she hit a wrong note. He never corrected her, only encouraged. "There's no wrong way to feel music," he told her once. "Just like boxing, your rhythm finds you."

Beyond music, she discovered other layers. Mark spoke fluent Mandarin, peppered with military slang. He understood Yiddish well enough to eavesdrop at Katz's Deli, and when he stumbled through Spanish trying to help a neighbor's abuela carry groceries, Boots burst into laughter so hard she nearly dropped the bag of onions.

"You're like a walking United Nations," she teased.

"I had a lot of layovers," he replied.

He would take her on walks past mural-covered alleyways in the Bronx and tell stories behind the brushstrokes. "This one," he said, pointing to a wall of swirling blue and red, "was painted by a guy who lost his brother at Anzio. Said putting color on the wall helped him breathe again."

Boots began to see the city through Mark's lens, a city of survival and quiet expression, stitched together by people trying to reclaim something gentle in a world that had gone hard. She started sketching again, small drawings of city scenes and music notes in her journal. With Mark, her world expanded. With Boots, his wound began to heal.

One night, after a slow dance in his tiny kitchen, she rested her head on his shoulder and whispered, "When I was little, I used to dream of a man who could make me laugh and cry in the same minute. You might be that man."

He kissed her hair and didn't speak. The silence between them didn't need filling.

Later that week, she left a note on his piano:

"You've given me music I didn't know I missed. Boots."

He tucked it into the lid of the piano and never told her he kept it there.

The church bells rang out under a cloudless Brooklyn sky on a warm June day in 1948. Mark stood at the altar, his hands calm but his chest thrumming like a snare drum. He wore a navy-blue suit instead of a tuxedo, not because he couldn't afford the rental, but because he wanted something he could wear again, something real. The same way he saw his future with Boots: not extravagant, but solid, lasting, stitched with purpose.

Boots walked down the aisle in a tea-length dress she designed herself, a veil that fluttered just enough to suggest wind even when there wasn't any. Her eyes met his and stayed there, not shifting, not blinking. Alex sat in the second row, dabbing at the corners of his eyes. Mark thought of that first pair of red gloves, the moment that started everything. It had led him to this.

The ceremony was modest but heartfelt. No orchestra. Just a string trio made up of friends from Alex's building. The priest, a former Navy chaplain who knew Mark from the war years, spoke plainly: "Marriage is not a ceremony. It is a daily choice. A daily honoring."

Afterward, they didn't head to a ballroom. Instead, Mark had rented a corner of Rockaway Beach near the pier. Picnic tables were dressed with checkered cloths. A friend's cousin cooked hot dogs and burgers on a large charcoal grill.

There was beer, lemonade, and a three-tier cake that Boots insisted was chocolate, no white cake nonsense. Their first dance was barefoot in the sand to a portable record player spinning Nat King Cole.

Boots leaned into Mark and whispered, "Let's never be boring."

"Deal," he said, his cheek against hers.

Mark had taken a new job with the city a few weeks earlier, an athletic supervisor for youth boxing programs and community gyms. It wasn't flashy, but it was meaningful. He would walk through the neighborhoods he'd grown up in and see himself in the eyes of wiry kids tossing jabs into the air. It kept him close to the ring but off the mat. Boots liked that.

But in quieter moments, he confessed to her something deeper: "I still dream of flying, Boots. I want to go higher, just not in planes anymore."

She had nodded. "Then build something. Build it here, in the city. Take kids who can't see past their corner store and show them the sky."

He looked at her as if she had just told him something sacred.

Their apartment in Brooklyn was small, two rooms above a cobbler's shop. But it was theirs. Mark would often return home late from the gym, smelling like leather and liniment, to find Boots sketching by the window. He would kiss the top of her head and say, "What did you dream about today?"

Some evenings, they'd walk to the boardwalk at Coney Island. Boots would carry her shoes and let her feet feel the wooden planks. Mark would buy them one bag of popcorn and insist she take the last handful. These were small luxuries, but they made their own kind of wealth.

They had no car. No fancy appliances. But they had laughter that could fill a room and silence that didn't sting. They had the piano. They had letters from the war folded between cookbooks. They had plans not yet spoken but already believed.

And Mark had a new dream. Not for glory. Not for medals. But for a legacy built in backyards, basements, and boys' clubs, where boxing saved kids the way it once saved him.

Boots would later say, "That June wasn't our beginning. It was our bridge." And neither of them looked back.

Mark Conn's entry into the boxing world wasn't just a passing phase or a nostalgic fling with the sport of his youth; it was the beginning of a serious new chapter, guided by one of the most legendary minds in the game. After officiating his first official bout in Queens, Mark was introduced to Ray Arcel, a cerebral and disciplined trainer whose reputation preceded him in the New York boxing circuit.

Arcel wasn't just training fighters; he was shaping the very essence of what modern boxing looked like, and now Mark would get a front-row seat to that transformation.

Their relationship was grounded in mutual respect. Arcel saw in Mark a rare combination: the raw instincts of a fighter tempered by the calm focus of a man who had seen real war. Mark, in turn, was drawn to Arcel's meticulous approach. Whether it was learning how to read the subtle shifts in a fighter's body language or understanding the importance of positioning as a referee, every lesson was a masterclass.

Mark often spent hours with Arcel between gym sessions, soaking in wisdom not just about refereeing but about the philosophy of combat, how to judge fairness without flinching, when to step in, and when to let the fighters work it out.

During these formative years, Mark's ringside presence grew more confident. The boxing community in

New York, tight-knit but fiercely competitive, began to notice the quiet but sharp-eyed official who never seemed out of place, no matter how chaotic the ring got. He didn't chase the spotlight. His integrity, timing, and fairness earned him respect without noise.

Outside the ring, Mark's growing involvement in the sport also meant a hectic schedule, city athletics work by day, gym sessions, and local fight cards by night. Boots, his newlywed partner, supported his ambitions, often attending matches with a small group of friends or waiting up for him with dinner and music ready. She called him "The Diplomat in the Ring", not just a referee, but a man with the power to keep tempers from boiling over, to calm fury with a steady voice.

More than anything, this chapter was about quiet growth. No headlines, no billboards, just a man showing up, learning from the best, refining his craft with humility. The streets of New York might have been loud, but in those moments beside Arcel, in crowded gyms and echoing locker rooms, Mark was listening to the rhythm of the sport, the heartbeat of a fighter, and the responsibility of the man who stood between glory and disaster.

By the late 1940s, Mark Conn had mastered the delicate dance of double lives, one in the bright fluorescent-lit offices of New York City's Board of Education, and the other under the harsh arena lights of the boxing ring.

By day, he was the respected Athletic Director overseeing school sports programs in Brooklyn, mentoring kids who needed guidance as much as they needed discipline. But when the sun dipped behind the city skyline, he transformed into the man in the bowtie and blazer, stepping into the squared circle as a referee, firm but fair.

It was not easy to juggle. A typical day might begin at 8 a.m. in a gymnasium filled with bouncing basketballs or echoing whistles and end past midnight in a smoky venue like the Sunnyside Garden or the Ridgewood Grove, calling bouts between hungry young fighters hoping for a shot at the big leagues.

But Mark thrived on the rhythm of it. Each role balanced the other; his work with students grounded him and kept his humility intact. Refereeing, on the other hand, sharpened his judgment, quickened his reflexes, and brought the thrill of live competition.

Boots, now his wife of two years, was both his anchor and his cheerleader. Though she sometimes worried about the toll these long nights took, she knew how alive Mark felt when he was around the sport.

She would help him press his shirts before matches and even took to watching film reels with him to study the moves of seasoned referees. They called it their "date night" ritual, one hand in popcorn, the other holding a notepad where Mark jotted observations like a student of the craft.

Conn's commitment didn't go unnoticed. Promoters began to request him by name. He had a way of keeping calm in chaos, whether breaking up clinches or calming hot-headed cornermen. His voice was low, but commanding. His eyes missed nothing. One moment, he'd be advising a young coach on playground safety equipment; the next, he was commanding respect from heavyweights throwing bombs in a ten-round war.

Sometimes the two worlds collided. Once, a high school teacher recognized him on TV during a local sports broadcast and later approached him at a school board meeting, stunned. "Mr. Conn, I didn't know you were *that* Conn!" The story spread fast, adding a layer of legend to his persona within the department. Students started asking him to teach boxing drills during gym class, and Mark, always game, obliged when time allowed.

Still, the double life wasn't sustainable forever. The hours were long, and sleep was often short. Mark began to develop systems to manage it all: daily planners, strict meal routines, and dedicated weekends for rest. Boots sometimes found him asleep with a scorecard in hand or dreaming aloud about a bout gone wrong that he wished he had called better. But she saw something else, too; this was not a man distracted. This was a man building something.

By 1950, Mark Conn was no longer a moonlighter. He was a name etched into the fight scene, even if he still clocked in with the Board each morning. His reputation was solidifying, fight by fight, and he carried himself with a mix of grace and grit that was hard to miss.

The dual roles, mentor by day, mediator by night, weren't just jobs. They were two sides of the same coin, and in both arenas, Mark was earning something far more valuable than money.

He was building trust. He was shaping legacy. And he was just getting started.

The bell echoed through Madison Square Garden like a starter's pistol for a new era in Mark Conn's life. Under the bright lights, with thousands of fans on their feet and millions more listening on the radio, Mark stepped into the squared circle, not as a fighter this time, but as the man in charge. It was September 27, 1950, and the stakes could not have been higher.

Joe Louis, the "Brown Bomber" and a retired heavyweight icon, had returned to challenge the reigning champion, Ezzard Charles. And right between them stood Mark, stoic, focused, and quietly honored. This was not just another bout; it was history unfolding in real time, and Conn had the best seat in the house.

The crowd buzzed with electricity, a mix of respect for Louis's legacy and curiosity about Charles's reign. Mark had trained for this moment not in the gym but in the small clubs and smoky rings of New York, developing an instinct for tension, timing, and fairness.

His sharp eyes missed nothing as he studied each jab, duck, and flurry. The fight was fast-paced, technical, and emotional. Louis, older and slower, fought with pride; Charles, crisp and composed, fought with something to prove.

As the rounds unfolded, Mark's presence was firm but invisible, a mark of a great referee. He separated clinches, monitored glove integrity, kept corners in check, and ensured the crowd saw a clean contest. In the twelfth round, when it was clear that Charles had outboxed the legend, the final bell brought applause tinged with bittersweet admiration.

Mark raised Charles's hand, a symbol of transition. The Garden roared, not just for the fighters, but for the man who ensured honor in the ring. This night carved Mark Conn's name into boxing's elite, and as the locker rooms emptied and the arena lights dimmed, he knew this was only the beginning of his legacy on the grandest stages of the sport.

Part III: Referee of the Golden Era

By 1951, Mark Conn's name was becoming a familiar one in boxing circles, but his proudest title had nothing to do with ringside fame. It was "Dad." That spring, Boots gave birth to their first child, a boy named Frank, named after Mark's own father. Two years later, their daughter Susan followed.

The apartment in Brooklyn that had once felt spacious now echoed with lullabies, rattles, and the soft thump of toddler footsteps. Mark often joked that the bell signaling round one had long since rung, only this time, it was parenthood that demanded his stamina.

He rose early, still keeping his day job with the Board of Education, where he now oversaw youth athletic programs with even more heart. Having children of his own changed the way he spoke to students. He saw their potential more clearly. He worried more deeply.

He advocated harder. His voice, once sharp and directive, now carried a note of gentle encouragement. "You've got it, kid," he'd say to a lanky boy struggling with a jump shot, hearing an echo of his own mentor, Alex, in the tone.

Refereeing remained a central part of his life, weekends, some weeknights, and the occasional travel assignment. But home was where his attention naturally drifted. Boots managed the household with humor and grace, yet Mark made it a rule to never miss the moments that mattered: Frank's first steps, Susan's first words, the annual family photo in front of the Rockaway Beach mural Boots had painted on their kitchen wall.

That wall, in fact, became symbolic, a mix of sea, sky, and dreams. Whenever Mark returned home from a fight, he would tap the painted lighthouse with his fingers before setting down his bag. "Still here," he'd whisper.

He never wanted to be the father who disappeared into his work. So, he made rituals. Sunday pancakes became sacred. Saturday afternoons were for bike rides or backyard catch. And bedtime stories?

Mark delivered them with the drama of a ring announcer, even when reciting *The Poky Little Puppy* or *The Tale of Peter Rabbit*. The kids loved it, and Boots would listen from the hallway, heart full.

Still, fame has a gravity of its own. By the mid-50s, more newspapers began featuring Mark's name. Reporters praised his "unshakeable composure" and "keen eyes." Coaches trusted his judgment. Promoters called him a "ref's ref", a professional through and through. And with that came more offers, more travel, more responsibilities. Mark learned to say no. Not every fight was worth missing Susan's school play or Frank's baseball game.

And yet, the balance wasn't always perfect. There were nights he returned home long after the kids had gone to bed. Once, Susan left him a crayon note on his pillow: *"I waited up, Daddy. You missed the story."* Mark folded that note and kept it in his wallet for years. It reminded him that his greatest corner was not in a stadium, but around the dinner table.

Over time, he began bringing the family to some local matches when appropriate, Boots with her ever-present sketchbook, Frank wide-eyed at the boxers' footwork, Susan mimicking ring girls with a scarf held high like a round card. Mark laughed, gently reminding her, "You've got bigger things to carry, sweetheart."

As the Conn family grew, so did Mark's foundation, not just in boxing, but in life. He was no longer just building a legacy in the ring. He was raising two futures, loving one woman with quiet devotion, and proving that greatness didn't require the spotlight. Sometimes, it lived in lullabies, pancakes, and crayon letters.

The night was thick with anticipation, the air in Madison Square Garden humming with the tension only a heavyweight clash could bring. July 12, 1951, Rocky Marciano versus Rex Layne. Two men entered the ring that evening, both hungry, both dangerous.

But it was the third man, silent, watchful, measured, who would walk away from that night with his reputation cast in iron. Mark Conn, once the quiet kid with red gloves in Brooklyn, now stood center ring, a trusted guardian of fairness on one of boxing's most brutal nights.

From the moment the fighters touched gloves, Mark knew this bout would be more than a technical match; it was a test of raw power and control. Marciano, already carving a name for himself with relentless aggression and compact dynamite in his fists, had that look in his eye: the glint of inevitability. Layne, younger and tough as nails, was no pushover. But this was Rocky's stage, and Mark sensed it early.

He moved with practiced grace, never in the way, always close enough. His eyes darted like a chess master's, tracking glove contact, elbow angles, the subtle shift of a fighter's foot that could mean a low blow or a slip. His ears tuned to the breaths, the grunts, the thud of leather on bone. And then came the moment.

Round six. A looping right from Marciano arced through the air like a wrecking ball and landed flush on Layne's jaw. The sound, dense, final, cut through the Garden's buzz like a bell cracking. Blood, sudden and violent, spurted from Layne's mouth, three of his teeth flying into the air. He staggered, arms flailing, eyes rolling up like a man watching his own stars. Mark was already in motion.

He slipped between the two men like a closing curtain. Arms raised. Fight over.

The crowd erupted in a mixture of awe and horror. Rocky's fans howled with triumph. Layne's corner rushed to the ropes, towels waving like surrender flags. Mark, calm amid the chaos, gestured for medical support and guided Layne gently to his stool. No panic. No flash. Just precision.

In the locker room later, a reporter asked Mark if he'd ever seen anything so brutal. He simply nodded. "It's part of the job. But safety always comes first. You let a man fall at the wrong time; you don't sleep at night." That quote ran in *The New York Times* the next morning, just below the fight recap. A small line, but one that turned heads in the boxing world. Mark Conn wasn't just a skilled ref; he was the kind of man you could trust with lives.

That bout marked a turning point. Promoters saw him as cool under fire. Coaches respected his consistency. Fighters, even those on the losing end, admitted they felt protected in his ring. And for fans, the image of Conn stepping in as Layne reeled, a steady figure in the eye of a storm, was unforgettable.

Back home, Boots had watched the broadcast on their small television set, flanked by Frank and Susan, who were too young to understand the violence but old enough to cheer when their father appeared on screen. "Look, that's Daddy!" Susan cried, pointing at the black-and-white blur. Mark walked in just after the rerun aired. Boots met him at the door, arms crossed, one eyebrow raised.

"Three teeth, huh?" she asked.

He smiled wearily. "Could've been worse. I called it clean."

She kissed him on the cheek. "Just don't bring your work home."

He didn't. Except in the quiet pride, the calm hands, the sense of justice that lingered long after the roar of the Garden had faded.

The night of September 21, 1966, carried the charge of something unpredictable. Madison Square Garden pulsed like a living creature, hungry, shouting, electric. The names on the marquee lit up more than just the street outside: Joe Frazier, the undefeated Olympic gold medalist with thunder in his left hook, versus Oscar Bonavena, the wild bull from Argentina with nothing to lose and fists like anvils. And at the center of it all stood Mark Conn, no stranger to pressure, no stranger to heat, but even he could feel the weight of this one.

Mark had been through it all by now; he'd seen champions rise and legends fall. But this fight had the feeling of two trains on a single track. No strategy, no finesse, just collision.

Round one opened with fury. Bonavena came out swinging, arms like pistons, surprising Frazier and the audience with a brutal flurry. Frazier stumbled, something nobody expected, and Conn instantly stepped closer. He was alert, eyes narrowing. He had to be ready, not just for a fall, but for chaos.

Bonavena's style was reckless, dirty even. His punches curved dangerously close to rabbit punches, and his clinches bordered on wrestling. Frazier, staggered but proud, dug deep. His corner shouted, the crowd howled, and Conn's whistle-straight posture never faltered.

In the second round, Bonavena struck again, this time a clean, blistering right to the jaw. Frazier hit the canvas. The Garden gasped. Conn stepped in, one hand counting, the other outstretched toward Bonavena to keep the distance.

"One… two… three…"

Frazier rose at four. No panic. No daze. Just grit.

Mark leaned in. "You good, Joe?"

Frazier nodded sharply. The fight resumed.

By round three, Bonavena's early fire began to fade. Frazier, slow and methodical, started to find rhythm. Left hooks began landing. Heavy, relentless. Conn could almost feel the ring shift under him from the pounding force. Sweat flew like rain. Blood dripped from Bonavena's brow. But neither man backed down.

The crowd was chaos incarnate. Some screamed for Oscar. Others chanted "Smokin' Joe!" Conn stayed locked in, wiping blood from his sleeve, calling breaks cleanly, separating clinches with firm, decisive hands.

Through rounds four and five, the momentum swung. Frazier knocked Bonavena down twice. Conn, calm and commanding, issued counts with ice in his voice. Bonavena beat them both, barely. But the writing was on the wall.

By the seventh and final round, both fighters were running on fumes. Faces swollen, ribs bruised, they dragged their arms into motion like tired warriors. Conn knew these were the hardest fights, not the clean knockouts, but the wars of attrition where the body gave out before the will. He watched their eyes, their footwork, ready to jump in if either man wobbled wrong.

When the bell rang, the roar of the Garden was deafening. Mark stepped between them, arms wide. Both men leaned on the ropes, breathing like steam engines. Cut men swarmed. Cameras flashed. And then came the decision.

"Split decision… Joe Frazier."

The room exploded.

Some fans erupted in joy. Others booed furiously. Bonavena raised his arms in disbelief. Frazier, ever humble, simply nodded. Conn stood firm, raising Frazier's hand. The spotlight hit them both, and Mark didn't blink.

Later, in the press conference, when asked about the controversial calls and the storm of opinions swirling in the air, Mark simply said, "I called it as I saw it. Fair's fair."

That line hit the headlines again. But behind it was decades of discipline, years of learning when to speak, when to step in, when to trust instinct over noise.

That night, Joe Frazier began his climb to world champion. Oscar Bonavena became a warrior in fans' memories. And Mark Conn, steady as ever, walked home, suit jacket over his arm, sweat-streaked shirt beneath, knowing he'd just officiated one of the fiercest bouts of the decade.

And he'd done it right.

The heat inside Madison Square Garden that July night clung to everybody like a second skin. It was July 12, 1950, one of those New York nights where the air barely moved, and the sweat on the walls could tell a story. The fans packed in shoulder to shoulder, buzzing with the kind of energy only a middleweight title bout could summon.

Jake LaMotta, the Bronx Bull, was defending his crown against Tiberio Mitri, the polished Italian contender with a surgeon's precision and a gladiator's pride. In the middle of it all stood Mark Conn.

Mark had refereed wars before, but this one felt volcanic. The contrast was stark: LaMotta with his brawling, battering-ram style, and Mitri with footwork as crisp as his white trunks. But boxing wasn't about aesthetics. It was about grit, damage, and endurance, and Conn was ready to oversee every second of the coming storm.

The bell rang.

LaMotta wasted no time. He charged forward like a man chasing a personal vendetta. Mitri tried to keep distance, jabbing and circling, but the champ absorbed the shots like an iron wall and kept advancing. Mark shadowed the fighters, silent but alert, watching their footwork, their eyes, the angle of every glove.

By the third round, LaMotta's face already showed swelling under the eye. But he never slowed. He walked through Mitri's punches like they were whispers and responded with thunder. Conn had to press himself into the ropes more than once to stay out of the action; these men fought like they didn't care who else was in the ring.

In round five, Mitri had a moment. He landed a sharp uppercut that snapped LaMotta's head back, drawing a gasp from the crowd.

Conn shifted his weight forward, eyes locked, wondering if a count was coming. But LaMotta only grinned, blood pooling at the corner of his mouth. He threw back three wild hooks that sent Mitri scrambling into the ropes. Mark stepped between briefly, tapping LaMotta's chest with a firm palm, warning him not to hit on the break.

Time passed like sand in a cyclone. Every round bled into the next, bodies colliding, gloves snapping into ribs, cheeks, temples. Mark could see the toll in their posture, the way each man sucked air through clenched jaws. But there were no fouls, no cheap shots. Just clean, brutal fighting.

By round ten, Conn's shirt was soaked through, not from nerves, but from the sheer heat of the Garden and the storm he was navigating. He glanced at his card during a clinch break: LaMotta had won seven rounds clearly. Mitri had taken two with clean movement, but his precision was being swallowed by LaMotta's relentless pace.

Round twelve. Mitri's footwork slowed. His jab dropped half an inch. LaMotta surged again. The crowd rose, sensing blood. Conn had to physically separate them twice to prevent shots after the bell.

He looked both men in the eye during the break, giving the warning that needed no words. This was war, but it would be fought within the rules.

The final three rounds were pure punishment. Mitri stayed standing, but barely. LaMotta battered the body, mixing in hooks with the rhythm of a man who'd fought every inch of his life. Conn kept the fight clean, but inside he marveled: this was history being written, punch by punch.

When the final bell rang, Mark raised both fighters' arms and guided them to the center. The announcer boomed the scores. Conn's card read twelve rounds to three for LaMotta. The decision echoed across the arena, unanimous. Jake LaMotta had defended his title, and the Garden roared its approval.

After the bout, Conn handed in his scorecard and quietly left the ring. His face was calm, but inside, he knew this one would live forever. A brutal ballet under hot lights. And once again, he had been the calm eye at the center of the storm.

The weeks following the LaMotta-Mitri brawl pulsed with headlines, but one name that kept surfacing wasn't printed across a championship belt or etched into promotional posters. It was Mark Conn, the referee. Quiet, precise, and controlled under pressure, he had become the talk of the boxing press. The phrase "the man in the middle" began appearing in columns alongside glowing commentary.

Sportswriters, fight promoters, and fellow referees alike were quick to praise what they called Conn's invisible command, a kind of discipline that kept chaos orderly without ever stealing the spotlight.

Mark had never sought fame. The ring was his workspace, not a stage. But after officiating a brutal, technically demanding 15-round championship like LaMotta vs. Mitri, his reputation expanded beyond the usual circles. One syndicated columnist wrote, "Conn has the rare gift of presence, enough to maintain control, never enough to interfere." Another called him "a shadow of fairness that follows the fighters without altering their fight."

To Mark, this recognition was a quiet vindication. His philosophy had always been simple: the best referee was one who enforced the rules without becoming the story. In a sport prone to drama and chaos, he believed in discipline, measured movements, steady tone, and sharp observation.

From the outside, it looked effortless. In truth, it required constant mental calculations: when to separate fighters, when to let a clinch unfold naturally, when a low blow was accidental versus strategic.

At home, Boots read aloud a glowing feature in the *New York Daily Mirror*, smiling as Mark poured his evening coffee. "'Conn displayed such poise under fire that one would think he was calling a chess match instead of a bloodbath.'" She chuckled. "A chess match?"

Mark shrugged. "I just kept the fighters honest. That's my job."

But those closest to him knew better. Behind that composed demeanor was a man deeply tuned to the emotional undercurrent of every fight. He watched more than fists; he watched eyes, breathing, hesitation, and intent.

He knew when a fighter was breaking inside even before the punches stopped landing. And yet, he never rushed in. Timing was everything. Authority had to feel earned, never forced.

His phone rang more often now. Promoters wanted Conn on high-profile cards. Journalists requested interviews, though he often declined. Younger referees asked for mentorship, eager to learn the craft beyond the rulebook. Conn gave his time sparingly but sincerely. He'd meet them at the gym or over coffee, emphasizing the same fundamentals: be fair, be firm, be invisible.

His old mentor Alex noticed the shift, too. One afternoon at Stillman's Gym, Alex leaned over the ropes while Mark observed a pair of featherweights sparring.

"You've got something rare, kid," Alex said, nodding toward the fighters. "They trust you more than their corners."

Mark smiled but said nothing. Praise always made him a bit uneasy. In his mind, the fighters were the story. He was just there to make sure the story stayed on course.

Still, it wasn't lost on him that his presence could change the rhythm of a bout. His calm energy defused hot tempers before they exploded. His subtle gestures reminded fighters of the rules without needing to shout. And above all, his consistency made him respected by fans, coaches, and even the toughest brawlers.

By the end of 1950, his name had become synonymous with clarity in the blur of fists and fury. To some, he was just a referee. But to those who watched closely, he was the anchor that kept the sport grounded, no matter how wild the storm inside the ropes became.

The morning light filtered through the lace curtains of their modest Mark Conn in his Brooklyn apartment, catching dust motes in soft suspension. Boots sat at the kitchen table with a cup of tea, scissors in hand, carefully trimming around another newspaper article.

It featured Mark's officiating at the Garden, his calm resolve under pressure, his name rising in headlines usually reserved for prizefighters and champions. She laid it beside a growing stack of clippings, already organized by year and bout.

Mark walked in from the bedroom, toweling his damp hair after an early jog. He paused when he saw her, head bent in focus, brows drawn together with quiet purpose. "You starting a scrapbook or a shrine?" he teased, setting the towel over the chair.

Boots looked up and smiled, tucking a lock of auburn hair behind her ear. "A little of both," she said. "Someone has to remember the details. The world forgets too fast."

At first, Mark had brushed it off as sentimentality. But over time, he began to understand. These weren't just newspaper clippings. They were markers of a life being built, not just his career, but their shared journey. Every article she saved, every margin she annotated with the date and location, was an act of love. A preservation. A quiet ritual.

She had started the habit after the LaMotta-Mitri fight. The press had taken notice of Mark in a new way, and so had she. Not because of the fame, but because she saw how the recognition made him stand taller, how it grounded him after years of hard work in anonymity. Boots had seen him juggle city jobs, night refereeing, parenting, and grief. She knew how much he carried behind that calm exterior.

So, she made it her mission to carry some of it with him.

The clippings lived in a leather-bound binder she kept on the bookshelf next to her music books. Each page told a story. Not just of knockouts and decisions, but of who Mark had been at that moment, what he was chasing, what he was balancing, what had changed.

They shared quiet nights in the living room, the soft crackle of the radio in the background, as she filed the latest articles and read snippets aloud. "Listen to this," she'd say, voice laced with pride. "'Conn displayed nerves of steel amid a sea of sweat and jeers.'" She looked up, eyes shining. "They get it now."

Mark would smile, humbly brushing it off. "They write what sells."

"But you live what matters," she'd reply.

Her rituals extended beyond the scrapbook. She pressed his referee shirts, laid out his stopwatch, and reminded him to eat before heading out. He learned to accept these routines not as coddling, but as anchors. Her presence was the one corner of his life untouched by the roar of crowds or the politics of boxing. She was home.

When Frank toddled into the room, Boots scooped him up, perching him on her lap. She pointed to a photo in one of the clippings. "That's Daddy at Madison Square Garden," she whispered. The boy looked wide-eyed, more interested in the sound of her voice than the image, but Mark watched the scene in stillness, a quiet warmth growing in his chest.

He wasn't one to talk much about legacy. But watching Boots carefully file another page into the binder, he realized she wasn't just saving memories. She was building a monument in motion. A living, breathing tribute woven into the rhythm of their days.

And in those simple acts of care, their love deepened, not with grand declarations, but with every crease folded, every headline saved, every meal left warm on the stove.

Chapter 8

"Break!" and the Boom of Ali (1970)

Madison Square Garden roared like a coliseum reborn, echoing with the thunder of thousands who came to witness Muhammad Ali's latest comeback clash. It was December 7, 1970, and across from him stood Oscar "Ringo" Bonavena, a thick-necked Argentine bruiser known for his unpredictable brawling and total lack of fear.

And standing between them, dressed in black, focused as steel: Mark Conn. The referee who had become synonymous with grace under fire, the trusted eye of fairness in the eye of chaos.

Conn had officiated many brutal battles before, but tonight carried the electricity of history. Ali, just months back from a three-year boxing exile imposed by his refusal to be drafted into the Vietnam War, had already made headlines in October with a victorious return against Jerry Quarry. But Bonavena was different. He was rawer. Hungrier. Dangerous. The Garden pulsed with tension as the fighters met in the center ring, and Mark raised his hand between them.

"Protect yourselves at all times," Conn instructed, his voice steady as the fighters locked eyes.

The opening rounds were slow and strategic, Ali dancing, jabbing, reading Bonavena's reactions. Bonavena, flat-footed but relentless, charged forward like a human battering ram. Mark kept himself just close enough, circling, sliding, his eyes flicking between their shoulders and gloves, always reading the rhythm of the ring. He knew this fight might not be beautiful, but it would be telling.

As the rounds wore on, Bonavena leaned into his unorthodox style. He ducked low, threw looping shots, and occasionally led with his head. Ali, showing signs of ring rust, began to talk more than he struck, taunting the Argentine with slurred mockery. And yet, the rounds passed with more clinches than combinations. The crowd grew impatient, then tense. It was not the ballet they expected.

By round 10, Conn had already warned both men for excessive holding and rabbit punches. He stepped in often, not to dominate the spotlight, but to restore the cadence of the contest. He would bark a sharp "Break!" and slice between the fighters with the precision of a scalpel, never allowing things to turn dirty. His voice had the weight of command without raising its volume.

Journalists would later say that Conn's control was the glue that held the bout together.

By round 13, Ali began to find his groove. Bonavena, durable but slowing, started missing wider. Ali's jab stung sharper. A straight right snapped Bonavena's head back, and the crowd erupted as if waking from a fog. Conn, watching carefully, knew the end was drawing near.

Round 15. The final round. And suddenly, it came.

Ali, seemingly conserving everything for this crescendo, exploded with a left hook, followed by a right. Bonavena's legs buckled. Another left. Another right. Bonavena dropped. The Garden erupted.

Mark Conn swiftly took control.

"One!"

He crouched, began the count. Bonavena struggled up, dazed. But the ref's cadence was clear. "Two! Three!"

By eight, Bonavena was up, but he stumbled toward the corner post, his eyes cloudy.

"Walk to me!" Conn commanded.

Oscar stumbled sideways.

Conn knew what to do. He waved it off.

The crowd exploded, half in relief, half in awe. Ali had won, but more than that, Conn had ensured that Bonavena left the ring on his feet, dignity intact, safety protected.

In the post-fight press conference, Ali gave his usual dazzling remarks, deflecting questions with jokes and poetic jabs. But even he paused at one point and gestured toward Mark Conn, who stood in the back with his arms folded.

"That man," Ali said with a grin, "he kept it real in there. He saw it. He called it."

Newspapers the next day praised the fight, but more than one column noted Conn's poise, especially during the volatile 13th and 15th rounds. "The referee is not there to win cheers," one editorial read, "but last night, Conn earned them anyway."

For Mark, it was another day in the ring. But privately, as he and Boots sat at their small kitchen table the next morning, he held the folded newspaper in one hand and her fingers in the other.

"Not bad for a night at the office," he said with a quiet smile.

She beamed. "You held the line again, Mark."

And he had. Between two titans, in the glare of cameras and chaos, Mark Conn had done what he always did best: make the ring safe for greatness.

Referee Mark Conn steps in as Muhammad Ali towers over Oscar Bonavena, who clutches the mat in pain during their dramatic 1970 bout at Madison Square Garden. Conn's steady presence ensured order in the chaos, embodying his role as the sport's quiet guardian.

The house smelled of cinnamon toast and aftershave. Mark dropped his gym bag by the front door and loosened his collar. The night's roars still echoed in his ears,

Bonavena's thuds, Ali's whip-quick jabs, the ringing bell, and the buzz of Madison Square Garden's lights.

But here at home, it was soft light, warm air, and slippers by the heater. Boots was on the couch in her robe, legs tucked under her, reading the *Times*. Her lips curved before she looked up.

"Well, if it isn't the man who faced down a thunderstorm of punches."

Mark chuckled and stepped in for a kiss. "You saw the fight?"

Boots nodded, folding the newspaper on her lap. "You were like a statue in there. Calm as the moon. And then, boom, fifteenth round, Bonavena hit the mat like a dropped sack of bricks."

"I had a front-row view." He smiled tiredly, pulling off his jacket. "Ali's sharp. And Bonavena wasn't going down easy. I kept thinking, 'One false call and I'm the story instead of them.' That's not the kind of press I want."

Boots raised an eyebrow. "You *are* getting press. They're calling you 'the man in the middle with nerves of steel.'"

He scoffed, walking toward the kitchen. "They should call me 'the man who forgot to eat before officiating fifteen rounds.'"

Boots followed him in, leaning against the doorway. "You missed dinner and bedtime. You know the kids waited up. Marty said, 'Daddy's going to be in the newspaper again!' And Rachel cried when I made her go to bed."

Mark's hand paused mid-reach for the kettle. "Damn. I hate missing them."

"You're doing your job. They'll understand, someday." Her voice softened. "But maybe... not this Saturday."

He looked up, puzzled.

Boots grinned. "There's a school play. Rachel has one line, 'Welcome, Great King!' She made you a seat with glitter on it."

He laughed, but the sound caught somewhere in his chest. "I can't let her down."

"No, you can't." Boots came over and wrapped her arms around his waist from behind. "You stood between two of the greatest fighters alive tonight and kept order like a lighthouse in a hurricane. That's something. But here, you're just Dad. And glitter seats matter."

Mark placed his hands over hers. The kettle began to whistle.

"I didn't start out chasing headlines," he said, almost to himself. "I just wanted to keep things fair. Clean. And now it's all flashing lights and interviews."

Boots kissed his shoulder. "Then unplug. Just for a day."

He turned, smiling as he poured two cups of tea. "Deal. No Garden. No boxing. Just the 'Great King' and her loyal subject."

As they walked back to the couch, Boots pulled something from under a cushion, a manila envelope.

"From Mr. Dundee," she said. Arrived this afternoon. Marked urgent."

Mark opened it cautiously. Inside was a photo of him from the Ali-Bonavena match, whistle in mouth, one arm raised, Ali stepping back, Bonavena mid-fall. Scrawled in blue ink across the bottom: *"You're part of history now, Conn. Next stop: Ali vs Frazier?"*

His brow furrowed. "Frazier..."

Boots tilted her head. "The FIGHT?"

"Yeah. Maybe. They're talking March."

She read his face. "Biggest event in the world. But... can you still be our Mark Conn, too?"

Mark set the photo down and pulled her close.

"I don't want to be famous. I just want to be *right* in the ring. And right by you."

She laughed into his chest. "Then start by being on time Saturday morning. Or face Rachel's wrath."

Mark feigned a shiver. "Now *that's* terrifying."

The kettle's steam faded. The house was quiet again, the Garden thousands of cheers away. But in the soft hum of the radiator, in the crinkle of construction paper taped to the fridge spelling "Go Daddy!", in the warmth of a shared couch and cooling tea, this was the legacy he wanted to protect. Not just the fights he called, but the love he returned to.

The apartment on 132nd Street pulsed with warm Sunday rhythms. Light slanted through the curtains like stage lights across a faded ring. Mark Conn sat beside a small upright piano, his large referee's hands spread over the worn keys like he was about to command another brawl into order. Only this time, the opponent wasn't a snarling heavyweight; it was a sticky D-minor chord that young Michael just couldn't get right.

"Try again," Mark said, gently. "Thumb under on G. Slide it, like a jab. Not too hard."

Michael grinned, tongue poking out in concentration. "Like this?"

The notes came out a little cleaner, and Mark nodded approvingly. His grandson wasn't a musical prodigy, not yet anyway, but he had rhythm. It ran in the blood, the way timing did for fighters. Mark believed rhythm had saved his life, inside and outside the ring. And if he could teach it to MJ, even just the feel of it, maybe it would save him, too.

Boots watched from the kitchen, apron around her waist, a pot of meatballs simmering on the stove. Her eyes sparkled at the sight of her husband, the "man in the middle," now taking the sideline for a different kind of lesson.

"Jazz is a conversation," Mark explained, tapping the keys softly. "Like refereeing. You listen, then respond. You don't yell unless you have to. You give space, but step in if it gets messy."

Michael looked up, puzzled. "Like when you say 'Break!' to the boxers?"

"Exactly." Mark chuckled. "Musics got its own 'breaks', and they matter just as much."

It was a far cry from Madison Square Garden, where just a week ago he'd stood between Muhammad Ali and Oscar Bonavena, commanding titans with sharp calls and even sharper instincts. That night, the crowd roared with 20,000 voices, but here, in this little living room, the only applause came from a delighted grandmother clapping in time.

"Ali kept clinching," Mark told MJ as the boy struggled through a few bars of "Take the A Train." "Bonavena wouldn't let go. I had to pull 'em apart again and again. Round fifteen came, and Ali dropped him. I had to kneel beside Bonavena to count him out. Not every day you see a man fall like a building."

"Was he okay?"

"Shook up. But yeah, okay. Ali hit hard. Real hard. But never dirty. That's why I respect him."

Michael stared at his grandfather like he was reading a comic book come to life. Boots handed Mark a coffee, then tousled her grandson's hair.

"Music first, boxing stories later," she said. "Let the boy learn rhythm before you teach him how to duck."

Mark winked. "One teaches the other."

As the sun slipped lower, Mark leaned back, watching MJ's small fingers stretch over the keys. He was getting better. Bit by bit. That stubborn LaMotta tenacity ran in the family, but so did something softer, Boots' calm, Mark's patience, the joy of a well-timed pause.

Later, when MJ went off to his room, Mark lingered at the piano. He tapped out a few bars of "Blue Monk," letting the melody swing. He wasn't a trained musician, not really. But he knew sound the way he knew breath and fists, knew when a note needed space and when it needed fire.

Boots came over and set her coffee down beside him.

"You ever think you'd end up here?" she asked. "Teaching a kid piano, after standing in the middle of world champions?"

Mark looked at her, smile slow and real. "I think this might be my best gig yet."

She leaned down and kissed his forehead. "Then don't be late for it."

In that moment, the ring lights faded. The roar of the crowd became a soft jazz melody drifting from a cheap piano. The legacy wasn't just in the Garden archives or newspaper clippings. It was here, in a boy learning to listen, in the stillness between notes, in the steady hands of a man who once called "Break!" and now called "Again, from the top."

The evening sunlight spilled across the living room floor like golden syrup, catching dust motes in its quiet stream as Mark Conn sat back in his recliner. A baseball game crackled through the radio, the announcer's voice rising with excitement as the Yankees chased another run. On the carpet in front of him, Frankie was sprawled belly-down, tracing baseball stats with his finger in the newspaper. "Dad, you think Reggie's really gonna break forty homers this season?"

Mark smiled, the edges of his mouth creasing like the well-worn gloves he'd tucked away years ago. "Kids got the swing of a switchblade," he muttered. "Fast. Confident. Maybe cocky." He paused. "Reminds me of a young fighter."

Frankie grinned. "Like Ali?"

"Like your old man," Mark chuckled, tapping his chest with a wink.

From the kitchen came the scent of fresh bread and the click of playing cards. Susan was sitting at the table with Boots, who was teaching her bridge. "No peeking at my hand, Missy," Boots warned, narrowing her eyes as Susan smirked.

"I wasn't peeking," Susan replied innocently, then whispered, "But Grandpa always leads with hearts when he's bluffing."

Boots let out a dramatic sigh and threw her hands in the air. "Traitor!"

Mark watched them from his chair, letting the domestic comfort seep into his bones. But sometimes, the quiet brought echoes. It wasn't always easy to shift from the booming crowds of the Garden or the roar of warplanes in China to this hush, bridge games, bedtime knock-knock jokes, and Susan's ballet recitals. He didn't regret it. He cherished it. But the adjustment had been no small feat.

Later that night, after the dishes had been stacked and Susan had brushed her teeth with exaggerated flair, she tiptoed into the bedroom with a flashlight and a frown. "Daddy," she said seriously, "Frankie says the Boogeyman hides in closets. But you used to fight real bad guys, right? So you can protect me?"

Mark looked down at her, eyes softening. "Susan, I've faced worse than the Boogeyman. I've faced angry heavyweights, generals, and referees who forgot their glasses."

She giggled.

He crouched and whispered like a conspirator, "But I'll tell you a secret. The trick is not being the biggest or the strongest, it's about standing your ground, no matter how scared you are."

Susan looked at him for a long moment, nodding solemnly. "Okay. But you'll still check the closet?"

He saluted. "Every night."

That was Mark Conn in the 1970s, not just a referee anymore, not just a war hero or a sportsman. He was a father figuring out how to balance the gravity of his past with the simple weight of being present. There were days when Frankie's little league games felt more nerve-wracking than a world title bout, and nights when Susan's innocent questions opened trapdoors in his memory. War. Fear. Fire. The faces of pilots he never saw again.

Boots had a way of anchoring him when those waves came. One night, when she caught him staring too long at a family photo from their early years in Brooklyn, she wrapped her arms around his waist and whispered, "They're growing up, Mark. And so are we."

Susan, Boots & M.J. Schultz

"But sometimes I still hear the engines," he replied, almost ashamed.

"And I still hear the crowd when you walked into the Garden," she said. "But here we are. Home. Real life."

He kissed her temple and nodded. She was right. She always was.

By the time summer rolled in, Mark was helping coach Frankie's team, taking Susan to piano recitals, and sneaking out with Boots for ice cream cones under streetlamps. Sometimes, when the stars came out and the house was quiet, he'd walk into his den, where his medals hung next to framed fight posters. He'd sit in silence for a while, then turn off the lights and go kiss his kid's goodnight.

The sunlight hit the edge of the easel just right, casting a diagonal shaft of gold across the living room floor. Susan, sleeves rolled above her elbows, stood before the canvas with a stillness that resembled prayer. She did not believe in chaos strokes or abstract bursts.

Her brush was slow, methodical; she painted the way Mark boxed: footwork precise, hands disciplined, eyes locked. When she added shadow to a cheekbone or light behind a flower's edge, it was not guessing. It was deliberate beauty, intention, not inspiration.

Mark paused at the doorway, a coffee cup in hand. He did not speak, not yet. He loved watching her this way, completely absorbed, unaware of the world. To him, Susan was a kind of quiet genius. She never called herself an artist, never demanded space. But when she painted, the entire household shifted. Even the kids lowered their voices as if something sacred was in session.

"You've been working on this one all week," he finally said.

Susan turned slightly, smiling. "She's almost ready." The canvas showed a woman seated on a train, face lit by the window, expression unreadable. Susan had captured that in-between moment, neither happy nor sad, just present.

Mark stepped in closer. "She reminds me of your mother."

"She reminds me of every woman who wanted more time."

He nodded. Susan rarely explained her work. But when she did, it was like unlocking a door that had been hidden all along.

Back when they were newly married, Mark struggled to understand her need to paint. It wasn't that he didn't respect it. He just didn't get it. Boxing was all about noise, cheers, bells, shouts from the corner. Her world was silent. It unnerved him. But over the years, he had come to see her studio as the place where things were not said but deeply known.

Now, he protected it like a guard at a cathedral.

"I'll take the kids to practice today," he said, sipping his coffee. "You keep working."

Susan tilted her head. "You sure?"

"Of course. You do not interrupt the artist during her storm."

She laughed, lowering her brush. "It's more of a drizzle today."

"Well, drizzle turns into a flood if you let it," he grinned, turning toward the hallway.

As he walked away, he remembered how Susan once painted a portrait of him, not in the ring, but sitting on the couch with MJ asleep on his chest. She'd used shades of rust and ash, making his calloused hands look like ancient stone. It was the first time he'd seen himself not as a fighter or a father, but as a man simply present. He had cried quietly in the garage, holding the finished canvas alone.

Boots later framed it and hung it in her hallway.

Susan returned to her work. Each stroke held weight. Every line whispered something only she and the canvas understood. Her painting was a ritual, not unlike his shadowboxing, rhythm, breath, repeat. It was how she kept herself anchored when the world tilted. And Mark knew that. That's why he never asked her to stop, even when the budget got tight or life got loud.

Later that evening, after the kids were asleep and the house dipped into silence, Mark tiptoed into her studio again. The light was dim; the air tinged with linseed oil. Susan had finished the painting. The woman on the train now had a book in her lap and a sliver of a smile. The whole piece looked like a memory you had not lived but somehow missed.

"She's beautiful," Mark said softly.

"She waited," Susan replied.

"For what?"

"For someone to notice."

Mark reached out and took Susan's paint-stained hand. He did not say it, but he noticed. He always had.

At the Conn household, the kitchen was always alive with sound. Sizzling bacon, the clink of silverware, and, above all, laughter. Frankie, now ten, was turning into a miniature version of his father in more ways than one. Not with gloves or grit, but with timing and mischief. While Mark once danced around punches, Frankie danced around words, delivering zingers at the breakfast table like a stand-up comic in training.

One morning, as Susan struggled to find her sketchbook and Boots stared down the crossword, Frankie piped up, "Why did the boxer bring a ladder to the ring?" He didn't wait for an answer. "Because he wanted to take his opponent to new heights!" Mark nearly choked on his coffee. Boots smirked over her reading glasses, not missing a beat. "Let's hope he remembered to duck the altitude."

The back-and-forth was relentless. Mark recognized in Frankie a gift he never knew how to nurture, humor as shield, humor as invitation. It reminded him of the soldiers in the Pacific. The best survivors weren't always the strongest; they were the ones who could laugh while holding a gun.

But it wasn't just Frankie shining. Boots was stepping into her own spotlight. Her evenings were spent less at PTA meetings and more at competitive bridge tournaments. She'd mastered the game the way Mark once mastered his footwork: not by brute force, but by reading people. Her strategy at the table was a quiet, dangerous thing. She knew when to fold, when to bid, and when to bluff you straight into a fall.

She played locally at first, then regionally. Soon, she was invited to a national tournament in New Orleans. Mark flew out with her, his first time attending one of her events, not the other way around. He watched as she sat at a felt-covered table in a crisp navy blouse, shuffling cards like a magician. Calm, poised, lethal. The scoreboard didn't lie. She placed second. One judge called her "The Conn who knows how to count cards instead of punches."

On the plane back, Mark held her hand. "You're the real champ, Boots."

She leaned into his shoulder and whispered, "About time someone noticed."

Back at home, the balance of power subtly shifted. Mark, once the whirlwind of the household, now observed from a quieter place. The kids respected him, but it was Boots they turned to when things got tricky, Susan for creative advice, Frankie for game night tips. Mark didn't mind. Not really. He loved that their family was becoming a constellation, not a solo star.

Still, he had his moments. Like when he walked in on Frankie doing impressions of Howard Cosell in the mirror. "And down goes Frazier! Down goes Frazier!" Frankie crooned, chin tilted, voice exaggerated.

"Nice form," Mark said, smiling.

Frankie turned, startled but grinning. "You think I could be on TV someday?"

"Kid," Mark said, kneeling to his eye level, "you already have better timing than half of them. Just remember,

comedy's like boxing. It's all about knowing when to hit…
and when to hold."

Frankie nodded, absorbing the wisdom. Then added,
"Also, always aim below the belt when Dad's not looking."

They laughed, loud and free. The kind of laughter that
echoed upstairs pulled Susan from her sketching and warmed
Boots as she read her bridge manual in bed.

Later that week, the whole family attended a local
talent night. Susan recited a poem she'd written about seasons.
Frankie told a series of jokes, including a harmless roast of his
parents that left the audience in stitches. Boots watched, arms
folded with pride, while Mark chuckled with glassy eyes.

When Frankie ended with, "And last but not least, I
want to thank my dad, for teaching me how to roll with the
punches," the crowd erupted.

Mark stood and bowed like a ham actor. "Takes one
to know one, kid."

In the car ride home, silence settled in the best way.
Mark looked around at his family, Boots, brilliant and sharp;
Susan, artistic and thoughtful; Frankie, mischievous and
magnetic.

He never fought for titles. He fought for them.

And in moments like these, he felt undefeated.

Part IV: The Final Bell

In the spring of 1974, Mark Conn stood once again under the hot lights of Madison Square Garden, a place that had become as familiar to him as the living room in his Brooklyn apartment. He had worked 219 professional bouts; each one logged in the notebook he kept under lock and key in his study. This night, though, would be his final officiating performance.

There were no grand announcements or televised farewells. That was not Mark's style. His exit from the ring, like his entrance decades ago, was marked by professionalism, humility, and an unwavering focus on the fighters, not himself.

The bout that night was clean, competitive, and uneventful, by referee standards, a success. Mark moved as he always had: economical steps, keen eyes, total control. At one point in the fifth round, a glancing hook caught the red-corner fighter off balance, and Mark stepped in, not to call a knockdown, but to steady the fighter and check his composure.

The crowd roared, not knowing the moment carried extra gravity. Conn's presence had become a kind of calm anchor in the storm of high-stakes boxing, and this quiet gesture was the culmination of a refereeing career built on trust, sharp judgment, and absolute integrity.

By the time the final bell rang and the winner's hand was raised, Mark felt a strange mix of relief and loss. His legs ached more than they used to. His ears buzzed a little longer after each roar of the crowd. But he had not lost a step in clarity, in fairness, in presence. The decision to retire wasn't forced; it was chosen. He knew it was time. "You've got to know when to step out before you become a hazard," he would say, quoting an old coach who used to say the same about boxers who didn't know when to hang up their gloves.

Mark Conn left the ring that night the way he'd always wanted to: uninjured, uncontroversial, and respected. He didn't wait around for applause. He left through the tunnel with his duffel bag in hand, his shoes dusty, and his face calm. In the locker room, the younger referees came to shake his hand.

One even asked for his advice on an upcoming title fight. Mark smiled, offered a few short words, and then left without ceremony. He was not sentimental in the moment, but later that night, he stood alone in his kitchen and looked at a framed photograph of him with Archie Moore. He raised a quiet glass of seltzer to it, then turned off the light and went to bed.

Retirement did not come with a rocking chair or silence for Mark. He remained deeply involved in boxing as an advisor, trainer, and speaker. He became a quiet legend among boxing purists, an authority figure in the truest sense of the word. Young referees would call his house in Long Island to ask for mentoring.

He never turned them away. If they were sincere, he gave them everything he knew. "Watch the feet," he'd say.

"The eyes lie; the feet never do. You want to know who's winning the round? Watch where the feet are going."

Though he had refereed fights in every major venue from coast to coast, he always spoke most warmly about his time in the Golden Gloves and his early pro years. He kept every fight program from the 1940s and '50s, neatly arranged in binders. He also kept the telegram from Gil Clancy offering him the title bout between Emile Griffith and Benny Paret, a fight Mark declined for personal reasons, one of the few he ever did. "I knew that fight wasn't right," he said once, years later, his voice low.

Retirement also allowed Mark to spend more time with his wife, Boots, who was thriving as a national bridge player by then, and their children, Frankie and Susan. He would attend Frankie's Little League games and sometimes be asked to umpire.

He was reluctant at first but eventually agreed, and unsurprisingly, brought the same integrity and eye for detail to the baseball diamond that he had to the boxing ring. One coach said, "You can't argue with Mr. Conn. He sees it before it happens."

In the quiet of those years, Mark's mind would often wander to his time in the war and to the friends he'd lost. He kept in touch with several Flying Tigers veterans, attending occasional reunions, though he rarely spoke much at them. He preferred to listen. He once said that combat taught him what mattered most: "Control, courage, and clarity under pressure. That's boxing. That's war. That's life."

He also wrote, quietly, privately, pages and pages of reflections on the fights, the war, the rules, and what he called "The Line." In his notebooks, he described The Line as the invisible threshold that separated violence from sport, danger from drama, justice from chaos. His job, he believed, had always been to patrol that line. To keep fighters safe. To uphold the contract of fairness that makes a fight meaningful.

Mark Conn never sought fame. But by the time the 1990s arrived, boxing historians began reaching out to interview him. They wanted to document his methods, his philosophy. He resisted at first but eventually gave a long interview to a small boxing journal in Brooklyn. "The ref is like a good tailor," he said in the piece. "If the suit fits, nobody notices him. If it doesn't, everyone's complaining."

By the year 2000, Mark was known as a grandfather more than a referee, a war hero, or a boxing judge. But in the photographs lining his living room wall, the history was clear. A young man in a flight jacket. A middle-aged man with a bowtie in the ring. A silver-haired gentleman holding his grandson while a framed copy of the 1951 Golden Gloves hangs in the background.

He may have stepped out of the ring, but Mark Conn never left the fight. Not really. He simply took the discipline, the courage, and the grace of his calling and carried it into every room, every day, every decision. That, to him, was the true victory.

By the mid-1980s, long after his final steps inside the roped square as a referee, Mark Conn had carved out a name synonymous with integrity, fairness, and clarity in a sport often haunted by scandal.

Though he had stepped away from active refereeing in 1974 after a staggering 219 professional bouts, the gravitational pull of boxing was hard to resist. In 1987, drawn by the insistence of state commissioners and fellow boxing professionals who still trusted his eye and instinct, Conn returned, this time not to officiate between the ropes, but to sit beside them as a judge.

Judging was a different kind of challenge. Unlike refereeing, where the authority is physical and immediate, judging requires stillness and silence, discipline of a different sort. But Mark's background gave him an edge. He had always approached boxing as a symphony of styles, a battle of wills and footwork, not just brute strength.

His ability to read a fighter's tempo, understand ring control, and differentiate between aggressive flash and effective technique became his calling card as a judge. Judges, especially in big-money fights, were often scrutinized, but Conn earned near-universal respect.

That reputation would be tested, and confirmed, during one of the most debated fights of the 1990s: the 1989 middleweight clash between Roberto Duran and Argentina's Carlos Ferreyra in Atlantic City. Though it never held the hype of a Vegas title bout, the fight had sentimental weight. Duran, a living legend near the end of his career, was trying to hold on to glory, while Ferreyra, lesser-known but hungry, brought relentless energy and awkward angles.

The fight itself was brutal and close. Duran opened strong, landing sharp counters and showing flashes of his younger self. Ferreyra, however, refused to fade; he kept charging, landing body shots and forcing Duran to fight every inch of the ring. By round nine, Duran looked tired; by round twelve, the outcome was anything but clear. When the final bell rang, all eyes turned to the judges.

Mark Conn's scorecard read 115–113 in favor of Ferreyra. It was the deciding card. The arena erupted, with cheers and jeers ricocheting in equal measure. The broadcast team immediately praised the integrity of the judging panel, especially Conn's even-handed round assessments.

While Duran's fans were stunned, many insiders agreed: Conn had seen what many had missed, Ferreyra's control of pace in the later rounds, his bodywork, and his consistent pressure. The New York Times praised Conn's card as "a model of quiet courage in the face of nostalgia."

That moment confirmed Conn's enduring place in the sport, not just as a man of the ring, but as a mind of the ring.

Over the next decade, Conn remained active in judging under the New York and New Jersey State Athletic Commissions. He was present at dozens of high-stakes matches, including preliminary fights for up-and-coming fighters who would go on to become household names. Never one for the limelight, he often turned down TV interviews, preferring to let his scorecards speak. Fellow judges frequently turned to him for advice. Promoters respected him. Fighters, even the ones he scored against, knew he was fair.

Perhaps what made Mark special was his refusal to become jaded. Even in his 70s, he watched tapes, studied fight footage, and kept up with rule changes. He'd scribble notes about new fighters, discussing their weaknesses and strengths with young trainers he mentored.

He believed boxing was evolving faster, flashier, but also risked losing its soul. He spoke often about the need to protect the purity of the craft: "A punch that lands isn't always a punch that matters," he once told a group of young judges-in-training. "You've got to listen with your eyes. Watch what's effective. Don't get distracted by noise."

He judged his final professional bout in early 2000. It was a light middleweight matchup at the Roseland Ballroom, a modest venue but one that always reminded Conn of boxing's true heart: the local fight scene, where dreams began or ended in six rounds. After the fight, one of the younger judges approached Conn, asking if he'd be back next month. Mark smiled, tipped his flat cap, and said, "I think I've said what I needed to say."

The commissions wanted him to continue. Friends pleaded for him to write a book. But Mark preferred fading out on his terms. He had spent nearly seventy years inside the world of boxing, from the gyms of Brooklyn to the stadiums of China, from the war-torn airfields of WWII to the corner stool of Madison Square Garden. His life had been measured in rounds and decisions, in victories and losses both inside and outside the ring.

Even in retirement, his legacy endured. Trainers cited his judging philosophy. Referees studied his posture and calm command. And when the Boxing Writers Association of America held its annual award dinner in 2001, it honored Conn with a lifetime achievement award. Mark, modest as ever, accepted with a short speech: "The ring gave me more than I ever gave it. But I'm glad I gave it everything I had."

That sentiment would be echoed years later in tributes, documentaries, and even in the words of fighters who barely knew him. For them, Mark Conn was not just a judge of fights. He was a judge of character. And in the wild, unpredictable theatre of boxing, that mattered more than anything.

By the early 2000s, long after he had officiated his final match and set down his judge's pen, Mark Conn's legacy began to crystallize, not in fanfare or flashy tributes, but in quiet recognitions that slowly swelled into something more permanent.

Sports magazines started running retrospectives on "The Golden Era of Boxing," and Mark's name was almost always there, etched alongside fighters, trainers, and arenas that defined generations. Yet unlike the brash champions and headline-hogging promoters, Mark's legacy was earned not with punches thrown, but with the calm command of a single word, "Break!"

That word had become his signature, shouted clearly and firmly as fighters tangled too close on the ropes or inside the clinch. Mark never barked or belittled; he projected authority with a tone that was sharp enough to cut through noise, but respectful enough to avoid ego bruises. For many fans, "Break!" was not just a command; it was a comfort, a promise that fairness still had a voice in the ring. It echoed through Madison Square Garden, Atlantic City, and small halls in Queens, threading through decades of boxing history like a rhythmic anchor.

The magazines noticed. A 2002 *Ring Magazine* article ranked Mark Conn among the top ten referees of all time, citing not only his composure and fairness but also his "rare ability to let a fight breathe while never letting it spiral out of control." A full-page spread titled *The Man in the Middle* featured a black-and-white photo of Mark stepping between two swollen fighters, one glove raised to enforce order, his face calm under the brim of his official's cap. "He never made it about him," the caption read. "And somehow, that made it unforgettable."

In another issue of *Sports Illustrated,* a feature on iconic fight moments included an inset box titled *Voices of the Ring.* Alongside legendary announcers and corner coaches was a quote from one of Conn's bouts: "Break! Keep 'em up, son." The writer noted that while punches got the crowd on its feet, it was Conn's voice that provided the rhythm and the rules. "He sounded like a teacher, not a tyrant," the piece said. "And he never lost control, not once."

Former fighters began telling stories in interviews, podcast episodes, and local hall of fame speeches. "Mark Conn saved my career," said one retired middleweight. "He stopped the fight when my eye was closing. I wanted to keep going, but he knew better. I walked away that night angry, but I walked away. That's the difference."

Fans remembered too. In online forums and comment sections, Conn's name would pop up in discussions about great refs. "He was old-school class," one user posted. "No chest-pounding, no drama. Just did his job and did it right." Others recalled being kids in the bleachers and watching him glide across the canvas, never tripping, always watching. "It was like he was dancing in there," someone wrote. "I still hear him shout 'Break!' when I watch old fights on tape."

For Mark, this slow wave of recognition was both touching and slightly amusing. He had never chased fame, never marketed himself as a brand, never tried to steal the spotlight. He had always believed that the fight belonged to the fighters. "The referee's job," he often said, "is to protect the fighter and protect the sport. If the crowd remembers your name, you probably did too much or too little. I tried to do just enough."

But even he could not ignore the growing affection people had for his work. At family dinners, Frankie would read out new articles that mentioned his father. Susan, always the quiet soul, painted a portrait of Mark in the ring, hands outstretched, expression resolute, that still hung in the den. And Boots, his lifelong partner, clipped every new mention and tucked it away in a growing scrapbook, the same one she had started back in 1950 after that first bout in Queens.

In 2004, a regional sportswriters' group invited Mark to speak at a boxing legends panel in Albany. He was hesitant at first, but Boots encouraged him. "They want to thank you," she said gently. "Let them." When Mark stepped on stage, the applause caught him off guard. It wasn't thunderous or explosive, but it was steady and heartfelt, a room full of writers, boxers, and fans honoring a man who never sought to be honored.

During the Q&A, someone asked what he thought his greatest moment was. Mark paused for a long time, then said, "It wasn't a knockout or a big fight. It was when a kid I helped coach wrote me a letter. Said I made him believe you could be strong without shouting, that you could be tough without being cruel. I think that was it."

In the years that followed, even as his health began to slow him down, the tributes kept coming. Local gyms hung his photo. A youth boxing program in Brooklyn named its annual sportsmanship award after him. Young referees wore black baseball caps with a subtle white "M.C." embroidered on the back.

Mark Conn never asked to be remembered. But the world remembered anyway, not because he demanded it, but because he earned it. One fight at a time. One voice above the roar. One clear, calm word that cut through the chaos: "Break."

By the early 2000s, the boxing world had faded into the background of Mark Conn's life, not forgotten, but folded neatly behind newer routines and gentler rhythms. One of the most unexpected turns in this post-ring chapter came with the shimmer of ballroom lights and the strains of old big band melodies.

It was Boots who first mentioned the idea, nudging Mark with her playful persistence. "We've got the music in our bones," she teased one evening, swaying to Glenn Miller in the kitchen. "Might as well learn to move with it."

The suggestion led them to the modest but warmly lit community hall in Queens, where Ben and Gloria Vitucci, retired performers turned teachers, held weekend ballroom classes for couples looking to rediscover the romance of motion. Mark, ever the reluctant showman, protested at first. "I spent decades moving backwards in the ring. Now I'm supposed to go forward in a tux?" But Boots smiled that familiar smile, and off they went.

The first few sessions were clumsy. Mark's steps were too square, his instincts still wired for pivoting, not gliding. Ben, tall and breezy in his ivory shoes, clapped a gentle rhythm as he guided Mark through a basic waltz. "Feel the lead, Mark," he'd say. "Don't command the step, invite it." Gloria, beside him, would giggle. "He's still refereeing out there! Let the music win this round."

But over time, something shifted. The patterns became familiar, the turns less stiff. The man who once stepped between heavyweight titans now learned to spin his wife gracefully under a Harvest Moon spotlight painted on the ceiling. Boots, ever light on her feet, became his favorite partner and his patient coach, whispering counts under her breath and tapping rhythm into his shoulder with two fingers.

They weren't trying to impress anyone. They danced for themselves, two people rewriting their movements after decades of anchoring each other through louder seasons. It became their ritual: Friday night class, post-dance coffee, and a slow walk home hand in hand, their bodies aligned by a shared tempo.

Mark, to his surprise, loved it. There was joy in mastering something new, even at this age. "It's not all that different from refereeing," he joked to Ben one night. "You've got to keep your balance, stay out of the way, and know when to break the clinch." Ben chuckled. "Except here, you actually get to touch the pretty lady."

They performed in the annual Fall Showcase as "Conn & Conn", the only couple over seventy. Wearing a crisp white shirt and a black vest, Mark led Boots in a slow waltz to "Moon River." The room clapped with warmth, but the biggest applause came from their children and grandchildren seated in the front row. Susan dabbed her eyes. Frankie grinned like a boy.

Boots called it *The Harvest Moon Waltz*, a title she scribbled in her scrapbook beside a photo of their performance, her in a flowing lavender gown, Mark beaming beside her. It became a symbol in the family, a reminder that life had second acts, third acts, even encores. "Most people hang up their shoes," Frankie would later say, "but Dad just swapped his boots for dancing ones."

Beyond the waltz, Mark's nimbleness extended into other spheres. He joined the local Toastmasters chapter, not to perform, but to share stories. His speeches were filled with humor and humility, tales from boxing halls and street corners, of fighters and foghorns and the strange poetry of Brooklyn mornings. His timing was impeccable, his delivery calm and steady. "I wasn't the champ," he once told a room full of young speakers, "but I was the guy who helped the champs play fair. That counts for something."

In that little circle of storytellers and retirees, Mark found a new kind of audience, not roaring crowds, but listeners who leaned in, laughed, and nodded. His tales of LaMotta's stubbornness, Ali's dazzling footwork, and the time a fan mistook him for a hat-check boy became part of Toastmaster lore. One member affectionately dubbed him "The Ringmaster of Words."

It wasn't just nostalgia. It was a reinvention. Mark, who had spent his prime navigating chaos with order, now choreographed his twilight with elegance and wit. The same focus that once locked onto flurries of punches now followed the arc of a dance partner's spin or the rising laughter of a well-landed punchline.

Boots, of course, was always there, his partner in step and in story. She curated his photos, organized scrapbooks, and encouraged every new venture. "You're more alive now than ever," she once whispered after a dance. "And not because of what you did, but because of how you keep doing."

Their friends began to joke that Mark had aged backward. "The man's dancing, public speaking, mentoring teens, and still holding a perfect posture," said one neighbor. "What's his secret? Refereeing Jack LaMotta?"

Mark would just laugh and say, "The secret is Boots."

It started with a dare.

At the local Toastmasters meeting, after yet another laughter-filled speech about his days in the ring, a member leaned over and said, "Mark, you ever think of entering the humor contest?" Mark chuckled. "You think they'd let a referee tell jokes?" But the seed was planted.

Boots encouraged it. "You've been making people laugh for decades, whether in the living room or the locker room. Why not try it on stage?" Mark waved her off at first, claiming he didn't have the time or the material. But the truth was, he already had both. What he lacked was the push.

That push came when he was selected, almost unanimously, to represent their Queens chapter in the regional Toastmasters Humor Contest. He was reluctant, even shy about it, but he accepted. "What's the worst that can happen?" he joked. "They throw in a towel?"

Mark approached the contest like he had any bout, quiet preparation, a measured strategy, and trust in instinct. He didn't rehearse in front of mirrors. He rehearsed in conversation, testing punchlines on Boots, recalling absurd moments from boxing, and polishing the rhythm of each sentence like footwork.

When the day of the contest arrived, the hall was packed with fellow Toastmasters, friends, and curious guests. Most of the other contestants were younger, sleek in their business-casual confidence, armed with power poses and rehearsed gestures. Mark walked onto the stage in a navy blazer, pocket square tucked neatly in place, and eyes that had once stared down ring legends.

He opened with a pause. Let the silence breathe.

"Most people know me as a boxing referee," he said. "Which means my job was to get between two angry men and try not to get hit. Kinda like marriage."

The room erupted. From that first line, Mark owned the crowd.

He talked about refereeing LaMotta: "He didn't punch as much as he *announced his intentions*, with his forehead."
About Bonavena's mouthpiece: "Popped out so many times, I thought it was trying to escape the fight."
And about Ali's footwork: "I've seen squirrels in Central Park with less energy."

But it was the unexpected turns in his stories that won the night. He wove in gentle self-deprecation, "At my age, every dance step feels like dodging a punch", and surprising tenderness, "The best left hook I ever saw? My wife is hitting the snooze button."

Every joke had truth, every story had rhythm. Mark knew how to play a room the way he once read fighters in a ring, timing the delivery, listening for breath, knowing when to pull back and when to strike. He didn't pace the stage. He stood solid, occasionally lifting a brow or tilting his head for effect, letting his words do the dancing.

When he closed with, "I may not raise championship belts, but I raise eyebrows at dinner with grandkids. That's legacy," the room gave him a standing ovation.

He didn't expect to win. Truly, he didn't. But when the judges announced, "And the winner of this year's regional Humor Contest… Mark Conn!", he laughed the loudest. He walked to the stage with a mock boxer's strut, pretending to duck invisible jabs. The crowd loved it.

Boots stood clapping in the front row, eyes shimmering. Susan sent a bouquet the next morning with a note that read, *still fighting the good fight, with punchlines instead of punches*. Frankie called: "Dad, you crushed it. I'm putting that trophy photo in the family group chat."

The trophy itself wasn't grand, just a golden microphone on a black base, but it sat proudly in the living room next to a framed photo of Mark at Madison Square Garden, calling the break between Louis and Charles. "One for the fists, one for the laughs," he said. "Balance."

The win brought more opportunities. Other Toastmasters clubs invited him to speak, sometimes for competition, sometimes just for joy. He never charged. "You don't bill for laughter," he told one organizer. "It's like oxygen, we're all better with it."

He became known as "The Ref Who Riffs," and even younger speakers started asking for tips. Mark always replied with the same advice: "Don't try to be funny. Be honest. The fun's already in there, you just have to let it breathe."

His humor had layers, stories laced with life lessons, jokes that hit like jabs but landed with love. People left his talks feeling lighter, wiser, and strangely nostalgic for a time they never lived.

At one event, a man in his twenties approached him, holding out a notepad. "Mr. Conn, that bit about Ali's rope-a-dope being like my college roommate avoiding chores? I felt that." Mark signed his name with a wink. "Stick and move, kid."

Back home, he downplayed the accolades. "It's not Madison Square Garden," he'd say, sipping coffee. Boots would smile over her crossword. "No, but it's the standing ovation that counts."

And in those moments, quiet applause echoing in his memory, the golden mic catching sunlight on the shelf, Mark Conn, the man who once commanded silence between giants, now commanded laughter. Not as a performer, but as himself. Just a man with stories, grace in his step, and a funny bone that never failed to win again.

It started as routine. Every Wednesday night, the kitchen transformed into their little arena, no gloves, no scorecards, just a deck of cards, mugs of chamomile tea, and two players who knew each other better than they knew themselves. For Mark and Boots, the bridge was never about winning. It was about the rhythm, the dance, the unspoken dialogue across the table. It was where their hands spoke what words could not.

Boots had been playing bridge since her schoolgirl days, a quiet prodigy in strategy and restraint. Mark, always more of a physical tactician, came to the game later, drawn in by her love for it and the gentle fire in her eyes whenever she held a hand worth playing. "If you can read LaMotta's left hook," she teased once, "you can learn to read my bid."

And so he did. Over time, Mark grew to love bridge not just as a game but as a private language between them. It was in the way Boots tapped the table after a successful trick. The way Mark furrowed his brow when holding too many diamonds. They shared a chuckle when both knew the other had bluffed. Their lives had once pulsed with arenas, travel, crowds, and the spotlight. But now, the quiet intensity of a Wednesday bridge match felt just as electric.

They played through holidays, through rainstorms, through recovery days after doctor visits. When Mark's knee ached, Boots brought a cushion for his chair. When Boots' arthritis stiffened her fingers, Mark shuffled the deck and dealt with exaggerated flair, whispering, "Your magician at your service." They didn't keep score after a while. They kept moments.

One night, after Mark had lost a close round, he laid his cards on the table and said, "That was a knockout." Boots sipped her tea, raising an eyebrow. "You forget, I watched you referee fifteen rounds with Ali and Bonavena. You can survive a bad hand." They both laughed. Her humor was dry, always just enough to draw out his grin.

The bridge gave them something sacred, predictability in a world that no longer moved as fast. As their friends' visits became less frequent and public engagements slowed, those weekly games anchored them. No matter what the headlines said or what hurt in the morning, they had cards. They had each other. And in that space, time softened.

Occasionally, their children joined, Frankie cracking jokes about Mark's "poker face" and Susan gently observing the strategic ballet. "Mom doesn't just play bridge," Susan once said. "She choreographs it." Watching them, the kids understood that these nights weren't just hobbies. They were rituals. A practice in love, patience, and presence.

Boots had a notebook, leather-bound and worn at the corners, where she recorded especially memorable hands. In one entry from 2003, she wrote: *Mark bid a reckless 4 hearts. I held back my chuckle until after the trick. He smiled when I took the game. Said it reminded him of our first kiss, unexpected but perfectly played.* It was more than a log; it was a journal of their bond.

Mark never matched Boots in technique, and he never minded. "She wins because she plays the long game," he said. "Same way she got me to eat spinach in 1960." But there were nights when Mark surprised her, reading a complex suit distribution or setting a trap she didn't see coming. She'd shake her head in mock surrender. "You do know this isn't the Garden, right?" He'd wink: "Same thrill, fewer bruises."

In the bridge, there was room for memory. Sometimes, they recalled friends who used to play alongside them, Ben and Gloria, who taught them ballroom steps, or Ed from Toastmasters, who never stopped bidding no trump even when he had no cards to back it. "We're the last of the original table," Boots murmured one evening, shuffling slowly. Mark reached across and squeezed her hand. "And we've still got game."

Evenings spilled into stories. Between hands, they reminisced about refereeing Duran, MJ learning piano, the time Boots almost missed a game because she was stuck in the snow delivering Christmas pies. These stories lived in the spaces between shuffles, reminders that their life together was always more about connection than competition.

And in those silences, something deeper thrived.

Once, when Boots missed a bid due to distraction, Mark didn't tease. He looked at her, eyes soft. "You, okay?" She smiled faintly. "Just thinking about that trip to Maine. Remember the inn by the water?" Mark nodded. "And the lobster that tried to escape your plate." They both burst into laughter. No need to return to the game just yet.

The bond they shared, card by card, became the soul of their twilight years. It wasn't about winning or strategy anymore. It was about staying tuned in, showing up, hand after hand. Just like they had done in every season of their marriage.

In their final years together, even when memory sometimes faltered, their bridge game remained strangely intact. Muscle memory guided the deals. Familiar cues sparked joy. Mark would reach for the deck, Boots would light the tea candles, and the rhythm resumed, soft, steady, unbreakable.

Because the bridge never broke.

It held through years, through fights and laughter, through parenthood and public life, through the loneliness of old age and the comfort of knowing someone would always be sitting across from you, smiling, saying, "Your bid."

The phone call came on a gray afternoon, the kind of day where the sky felt too heavy even before the news arrived. Susan had been ill for months, her quiet strength carrying her farther than anyone expected, but when the call finally came, it still felt unreal. Mark stood by the kitchen window as Boots answered, the soft murmur of her voice slowly collapsing into silence. When she hung up, she didn't speak. She simply leaned into him, her forehead against his chest, and he understood without hearing a word. Their daughter, gentle, steady, precise Susan, was gone.

For a long moment, Mark didn't move. His breath came shallow, and a strange numbness crawled through him. He had seen death before, in the ring, in wartime skies, in hospital rooms where old friends slipped quietly away. But this was different. This was a piece of his life, his heart, his history.

A daughter who had once held his hand at bedtime, who painted with the same discipline she learned from him, who whispered jokes that only the two of them understood. Nothing prepared him for the kind of grief that steals the air from your lungs.

The house fell into a soft hush in the days that followed. Boots moved through the rooms like someone trying to remember the choreography of a familiar dance but finding each step altered. Frankie visited often, his humor muted. Boxes of Susan's paintings, journals, and photos arrived from her apartment, stacked neatly in the living room until the family could bear to open them.

The funeral was small, intimate. The kind Susan would have wanted. Friends from her art community spoke about her patience, her precision, her kindness. One described her as "the quietest storm", a presence felt deeply, if not loudly. Mark listened, his hands folded, his posture straight in that old referee way, shoulders back, feet grounded, as if only structure could keep him from falling apart.

When it was his turn to stand, he hesitated. Public speaking had come easily to him in his later years, humor contests, library talks, and Toastmasters gatherings, but this was different. This was personal. Raw. He stepped to the front and looked at the small gathering. The room blurred for a moment. Then he began.

"Susan never tried to be someone she wasn't," he said quietly. "She didn't chase applause or attention. She just did things right. Thoughtfully. Patiently. The way she painted… it wasn't just art. It was how she lived." He paused, swallowing hard. "She taught me to slow down. Even when I didn't listen." A tremor moved through his voice. "I hope she knew she made me proud. Every day."

He sat down slowly, Boots taking his hand. They didn't speak for a long time. They didn't need to.

After the funeral, people returned to their routines, as people do. But for Mark and Boots, life felt rearranged. Certain objects in the house became heavier: Susan's framed watercolor by the staircase, the birthday card she had written last year in her graceful script, the soft shawl she once forgot on their couch. Grief settled into the quiet spaces, not loud, not dramatic, but persistent.

Mark changed, too, though subtly. He spoke less. His famous quick humor softened at the edges. But he never disappeared into himself. He kept showing up at bridge nights, at community talks, at Toastmasters. Not because he felt strong, but because he understood that life didn't pause for heartbreak. It kept moving, asking gently for participation.

In the evenings, he sometimes sat in his recliner with one of Susan's sketchbooks resting on his lap. Boots would join him with tea, and they would go through the pages slowly. Landscapes with tight brushstrokes. Portraits with patient shading.

In many of them, Mark noticed details he had never seen before, a softness around the eyes, a calm in the composition, a quiet resilience threaded through every line. "She saw the world better than we did," Boots whispered once. Mark nodded, though words felt too fragile.

He kept her memory alive in quiet ways. He replaced the painting in the hallway with one of her favorites, an abstract swirl of blue and gold that she said reminded her of "movement inside stillness."

He brought a small watercolor to the next Toastmasters meeting and told a gentle story about the time Susan tried to teach him how to identify color gradients. "She told me I see in black and white," he joked softly, "and I said that's because boxing never gave me much else to look at." The room laughed, but they also felt the weight beneath the humor.

Sometimes, on mornings when the grief felt heavier, Mark took long walks. Not fast, not purposeful, just slow steps around the block, breathing in the air, letting memory settle and lift, settle and lift. He thought often of her steady presence, the way she observed the world with quiet gratitude. He tried, in his own way, to do the same.

Boots grieved differently. More openly at times, more privately at others. She and Mark moved through their loss in parallel lines, sometimes meeting, sometimes walking separately, always returning to each other by evening. Their bridge games became gentler. Sometimes they didn't finish a hand. Sometimes they did. It didn't matter.

What mattered was that they kept showing up. For themselves. For each other. For the daughter whose absence became a quiet shadow that walked with them.

Susan's passing marked one of the deepest losses of their lives. But in the way Mark rose each day, soft-spoken, steady, present, there was a quiet testament to the resilience he had carried since his youth. A resilience forged in Brooklyn streets, war-torn skies, Madison Square Garden crowds, and now in the aching silence of grief.

He did not stop living.

Because she had lived.

And that love did not end.

The quiet dissolution of Mark and Boots' romantic relationship came not with fireworks, but with the soft, knowing silence of two people who had lived and loved deeply. It happened gradually, marked not by arguments or betrayals but by life's gentle shifts, the kind that arrive with age, reflection, and the evolving rhythms of companionship. They did not call it a breakup. There was no need for such finality. Instead, it was an unspoken understanding: that their bond had changed shape, but not strength.

Boots moved into a separate unit in Palm Aire, a space filled with soft lighting, classic jazz, and her signature warmth. Mark helped her unpack, hanging her framed photos and organizing her books, just as he had done decades earlier when they first merged their lives. There were no tears. Just the comfort of touch and the occasional shared glance that said, "We did well."

Every Tuesday and Thursday, they were still seated across from each other at the bridge table, Boots' sharp eyes and Mark's measured calm making them a formidable team. Other couples around them whispered in admiration, not only for their card skills, but for their serenity, their unspoken language, their refusal to let go of something sacred simply because the form had shifted.

In the quiet hours, Mark would sometimes remember their early dances, their laughter over seafood dinners, and the time they had almost married but chose instead to remain free and loyal in their own way. He missed the intimacy but not the routine. He missed her scent on his pillow but not the arguments over clutter. And she, too, felt a nostalgia tinged with peace rather than pain.

They still called each other with news, jokes, and worries. When Susan passed, Boots held Mark's hand at the funeral. When Boots had a minor fall, Mark drove her to the doctor and waited outside with a thermos of coffee and a crossword puzzle.

Their separation was never about distance; it was a quiet redefinition. They were no longer lovers, but they remained each other's constants. Not everyone understood it. But those who had truly lived, who had lost and loved, who had weathered decades, understood it perfectly. Their friendship was a triumph, not a consolation.

At Palm Aire, the staff knew them as "the bridge partners," but those who paid attention saw something more profound: two souls who had chosen to walk alongside each other, just not in the same lane.

In the quiet stillness of his Palm Aire apartment, Mark Conn felt the clock ticking louder than ever. The aches came more frequently, and the naps stretched longer. Yet, he never complained. He still shuffled to the clubhouse for bridge games with Boots, even when his hands trembled. Word got around that the old champ wasn't doing so well. That news reached Frankie, now a grown man with a young family of his own.

Frankie flew in with his two children, bright-eyed, curious, and full of life. When they entered Mark's living room, the old referee lit up with a joy that hadn't touched his face in weeks. He struggled to his feet, ignoring the pain, and pulled them into a gentle hug. "So, these are the rookies?" he joked, eyes glassy. He asked their names twice, savoring the syllables, then introduced them proudly to everyone at the bridge table as "my grandkids."

He told them stories, about Madison Square Garden, about the war, about flying over China, and dancing with Boots under moonlight. The kids listened wide-eyed, unsure where truth ended and legend began, but wholly mesmerized by the twinkle in Mark's eyes. Frankie watched in silence, holding back tears.

For a few days, the room was filled with laughter, love, and warmth, like the final rounds of a well-fought bout, where the fighter knows he has nothing left to prove. Mark smiled when they left, his voice soft: "Tell 'em they made their old grandpa proud."

And in that moment, the fighter, the flier, the referee, Mark Conn, sat still, surrounded by his memories, ready for the last bell.

The hospital room was quiet in a way Mark had never known before. For a man who had lived in the roar of boxing crowds, the drone of fighter planes, the bustle of New York schoolyards, and the lively chatter of Palm Aire bridge tables, this stillness felt unfamiliar.

The monitor beside him beeped in a slow, steady rhythm, each sound marking the passing of another moment. It was September 29, 2011, and Mark Conn, who had survived war, championship bouts, and nearly a century of life, was entering the final round of a fight he could no longer

control.

Mark Conn refereed many championship fights in his career.

Boots sat on the edge of his bed; her hand wrapped gently around his. Age had softened both of them, but her presence remained as steady as it had been in their youth, when she painted murals at Silver Gull and he showed off piano melodies to win her smile. They had gone through chapters that lovers, friends, and companions rarely navigate as gracefully: romance, separation, reconnection, partnership, and the long companionship that forms when two people have shared more decades than most marriages survive.

She looked at him now with eyes that held every memory: the first spark, the years of bridge games, the dances, the nights celebrating after big fights, the sorrow of losing Susan, and the quiet understanding that their bond had never truly broken.

Mark's breathing was shallow, each inhale a fragile lift, each exhale a reminder of the body's slow surrender. Boots leaned closer, brushing a light hand over his forehead. "You don't have to fight this one," she whispered, her voice unsteady but tender. She had watched him fight so many battles, some in the ring, some in the air, some in the private spaces of his own heart. But this battle was different. This one did not require courage or footwork or the stern calm he had carried through Madison Square Garden. It required release.

Frank had been there earlier with his children, giving Mark a final glimpse of the family that had grown from a single marriage in 1948. The visit had exhausted him, but it had also filled the room with the warmth he had always carried for his son.

When they left, Mark had squeezed Frankie's hand harder than expected, as if passing something unspoken between them. Frankie understood. He had walked out fighting his own tears, knowing the next call would be the last.

Now the room held only Mark and Boots, two lives intertwined across seventy years, sitting in a silence weighted with affection, grief, and gratitude. Boots hummed softly, one of the tunes Mark used to play on the piano, a simple melody that had echoed through their Rockaway home and later through the halls of Palm Aire.

Even when her voice cracked, she kept going, holding the moment together with music the same way he had held life together with humor, discipline, and a constant desire to make others smile.

Mark's eyes fluttered open briefly, faint but full of recognition. He tried to speak, but the effort was too much. Instead, he gave her a small look, one she had seen countless times: after war stories, after tough matches, after quiet nights sitting together. It was the look that meant he was grateful she was there.

Boots squeezed his hand again. "It's all right, Champ," she whispered, the old nickname returning without hesitation, "you've given enough."

The beeping slowed, the rise and fall of his chest softened, and the air in the room grew still. Boots leaned down, resting her forehead against his. She felt the final breath, the gentle release of a man whose life had been defined by motion, finally coming to rest.

The final bell had rung. Mark Conn, the boy from Brooklyn, the Golden Gloves champion, the Flying Tiger, the celebrated referee, the bridge partner, the father, the friend, was gone. And Boots remained beside him, holding his hand until the room grew quiet again, honoring him in the only way she knew: by staying.

The sun glinted off the flagpoles as rows of veterans in pressed uniforms lined the funeral route. Boots stood still among them, her gloved hands clenched at her sides, the chill in the September air no match for the cold absence swelling inside her. Mark Conn, war hero, referee, father, fighter, had fought his final round. Now, those who had known his courage and character gathered at the cemetery to say goodbye.

The flag on his casket had been folded with reverence, every crease sharp, every movement synchronized. Frankie stood beside his mother, dressed in his father's favorite leather jacket, clutching Mark's worn flight patch from the Flying Tigers era. Conn's grandchildren, whom he'd once lifted into the boxing ring for fun, now stood quiet, one of them barely able to hold back tears as the honor guard raised their rifles.

The crack of the 21-gun salute shattered the silence. With each blast, it was as if the air itself paid tribute to the force of a life fully lived. For Boots, each shot echoed a memory: their laughter in the kitchen, the slow dances in the living room, his steadfast hand in hers during all those years of rebuilding after the war.

A bugler stepped forward, the notes of "Taps" soaring into the sky, carried by the breeze through the trees.

Faces turned upward, some hiding tears, others letting them fall freely.

Boots watched as the tri-folded flag was handed to her. The soldier knelt, offering it with the practiced words: "On behalf of a grateful nation…" But it was not the nation she heard in those words; it was Mark's voice, somehow still with her, in the wind, in the hush that followed the last note.

She did not cry. Not then. She simply whispered, "Rest now, Champ."

The boxing world paused. News of Mark Conn's passing swept through sports networks, local gyms, veterans' halls, and Madison Square Garden itself. To those who had known him in the ring, he was more than a referee; he was the invisible force keeping balance between glory and chaos. The man in the middle, standing firm between fists and fury, had made his final call. And now, across generations and borders, people stood in tribute to the legacy he left behind.

Frankie sat at his kitchen table; his father's Marine cap placed gently on the counter beside a stack of letters. Some were handwritten by former fighters. Others typed, from boxing journalists or gym owners who remembered the way Mark used to tip his cap before stepping into the ring.

He read one aloud: "Mr. Conn didn't just call the fights fair, he made them feel sacred." Another simply read, "He saved my life once by stopping a fight I didn't know I was losing. Thank you, ref."

At the Palm Aire community center, the staff had created a tribute board. Photos of Mark in his referee uniform, arms extended between champions, were pinned beside candid shots of him grinning beside Boots after a dance, or helping an elderly friend onto the shuffleboard court. A simple banner above the display read: "Mark Conn: Champion of the Ring and of the Heart."

Boots arrived with a bouquet of white lilies and a trembling smile. "He would've laughed at all this fuss," she said softly, her voice catching. But her eyes sparkled with pride. A small boy tugged at her hand, a neighbor's grandson. "He was the man on TV, right?" the boy asked. She nodded. "Yes, darling. The man who kept things fair."

A segment aired on ESPN Classic, replaying moments of Mark's most famous bouts, the Ali fights, the Hagler fights, the epic title defenses where his calm presence often became the unsung thread holding legends together. The commentary was respectful, filled with admiration. "He was never the story," the voice-over said, "but every great story in the ring had him standing in it."

In New York, at a quiet corner of Gleason's Gym, an old speed bag was marked with black ribbon. Fighters, young and old, bowed their heads. "He was one of us," murmured a retired heavyweight. "A warrior who didn't throw punches, but stood with the same courage."

Meanwhile, tributes poured in from the military community. Fellow Marines saluted, recounting stories from China, from the dusty airfields, from barracks filled with noise and fear. They remembered Mark as the one who kept calm when things went sideways, who stood tall for the lost and missing. His wartime letters, now shared by Frankie online, became beacons of humanity in digital form, poignant reminders of duty, humor, love, and hope.

The memorial service was standing room only. Veterans in dress blues. Fighters in sharp suits. Fans wearing old event tees with sweat-faded prints. Boots sat beside Frankie, who placed Mark's referee whistle gently atop the flag-draped table. A montage played, set to Billie Holiday and Duke Ellington, echoing the music Mark loved most.

A priest read aloud: "Blessed are the peacemakers," pausing to let the weight of it settle. Then he added, unscripted, "And blessed are those who stand in the middle and keep others from harm." The room stirred with emotion.

Afterward, as people filed out, many stopped to touch the display table. One young boxer, barely twenty, whispered, "I never met him, but I learned from him. You don't have to be loud to be strong."

Frankie looked up at the photo above the table, Mark with arms outstretched, halting two champions in mid-swing. The man in the middle. Holding back chaos with quiet authority.

"He always knew when to step in," Frankie murmured. "And when to step back."

Boots touched his arm. "And he always left with grace."

The world remembered. And so did they.

At a tucked-away comedy club in Sarasota, the lights dimmed as Frankie Conn stepped onto the stage. He wore a blazer over a tee, silver hair tousled like he had just walked in from a Florida storm. The mic crackled, the spotlight warmed, and the room settled. He didn't open with a joke. Instead, he started with a name.

"My father," he said, pausing, "was the only man I ever saw step between Muhammad Ali and Joe Frazier and live to talk about it."

Laughter. The good kind, the kind that says: we're listening.

Frankie grinned. "He was also the only referee I know who could yell 'Break!' and make two men with fists the size of Florida cantaloupes actually listens. I tried that once on my teenage daughter. She hit me with a rolled-up yoga mat."

More laughter. And with it, a heartbeat. Mark Conn's memory, pulsing gently through the crowd.

Frankie had never tried to be his father. That was impossible. But what he had, what his father had gifted him like a secret heirloom, was the rhythm of a good pause. A well-timed joke. The courage to command a room, not with noise, but with presence. Every set he performed, whether in Florida or Brooklyn or at a Toastmasters reunion, carried whispers of Mark's cadence, his restraint, his grace under fire.

Back home, Frankie ran a modest Oriental rug shop, something as old-fashioned and stubbornly beautiful as his dad's handwritten letters. Customers came in for floor art and left with stories. He'd roll out a Kazakh runner and say, "This one? Tougher than Rocky Marciano. Stood up to two cats and a Roomba. No KO."

He'd hold up a faded Turkish kilim and grin: "My dad refereed 219 fights. This rug has survived more dinner parties than that."

And people would laugh. But they'd stay. Because what they really came for wasn't the rugs, it was the legacy being woven between threads.

Some days, he'd bring out the old photos. Mark with Ali. Mark with Sugar Ray. Mark and Boots were at a wedding, dancing as if the floor belonged to them. One framed shot sat behind the register, Mark standing between two raging fighters, hand out, mouth open, mid-command. Under it, Frankie had taped a simple caption: *Fairness doesn't flinch.*

Boots stopped by the shop every so often. They'd share coffee in mismatched mugs and argue about Sinatra vs. Bennett, or retell the time Mark tripped on a ballroom floor and spun it into a bow. She never remarried. "How do you follow up the main event?" she'd say, eyes twinkling.

Frankie's children had grown up hearing bedtime stories about boxing, not the punches, but the pauses. The moments their grandpa had stepped in, looked a champion in the eye, and made him wait. "That's power," Frankie would say. "Not swinging. Knowing when not to."

When asked once if he'd write a book about his father, Frankie shook his head. "Nah., I tell stories instead. You can close a book. But a good story walks out with you."

And he kept telling them.

At open mics. Over bridge games. In the back of the shop, he tied knots on antique fringe. With each laugh, each shared memory, he kept Mark Conn alive, not in marble statues or dusty trophies, but in the breath and voice of real people remembering.

The man in the middle was gone.

But the man behind the mic, his son, was making sure the story never ended.

Sunlight filtered through the window panes of the Palm Aire community center, catching on the soft brushstrokes of a half-finished canvas. Boots sat in her usual spot by the east wall, where the light was just right and the breeze from the fan kept her paints honest. She leaned over the canvas, her hand steady, her mind quiet. Across the room, her bridge partner waited with a shuffled deck, smiling patiently. They never started a game until Boots put down the brush.

Today's painting showed two hands, open, mid-motion, reaching between two figures frozen in combat. No faces. Just shoulders, gloves, the raw posture of aggression paused by a calm, commanding gesture. Her brush hovered, then tapped the canvas with a final dab of shadow behind the left glove. Done.

She sighed. "Mark would've said, 'A little more space between the fighters, Boots.'" Her smile was soft. "And he'd be right."

Boots never stopped loving him, not in the loud way of novels or movies, but in the way she poured coffee into a chipped mug he once used, or corrected her bridge students with a raised eyebrow that was all his. After he passed, she taught more art. More bridge. More grace. Each lesson quietly echoed the man she had shared a life with.

Her students loved her. Not just for her precision or her patience, but for the way she carried stories inside silences. She would guide a trembling hand with a firm grip, whisper, "Slow down. Wait for the space. Then decide." Just like Mark in the ring.

When young players fumbled at bridge, she never scolded. She'd just tilt her head, shuffle the cards again, and say, "Even the champ gets dealt a bad hand sometimes. The skill is in the next move."

In the hallway of her condo hung a small collection: paintings of moments only she and Mark had lived. A pair of dance shoes resting beside a referee's whistle. A young Frankie with his first rug rolled open like a scroll. A watercolor of Madison Square Garden, not the fighters, just the empty ring and spotlight, waiting. Her favorite was simple: two chairs on their back patio, coffee cups untouched, as if the conversation had just been paused.

She didn't go around calling herself "the widow of Mark Conn." That wasn't her style. But when neighbors asked about the old black-and-white photo on her fridge,

Mark raising Ali's glove in victory, she'd chuckle and say, "He had the best seat in the house."

They had parted ways once, after Susan's death. Too much grief, not enough words. But never bitterness. And eventually, they found their way back, not as husband and wife, but as companions bound by memory, cards, and the art of knowing when to speak and when to hold.

Her bridge club was small but steady. Every Tuesday and Friday, she played with the same group, and every now and then, someone would slip and call her partner "Mr. Conn." She never corrected them. She just smiled.

She began painting more teaching aids, too. Watercolors that illustrated card combinations. Acrylics that showed bridge tables under dreamlike skies. Art, like a bridge, became her language for staying close to him. Each canvas held a whisper: of discipline, of humor, of love that knew how to last through change.

On a warm afternoon, one of her students, a young girl from the neighborhood, stayed after class. "Miss Boots," she asked, "was your husband famous?"

Boots didn't flinch. She looked down at her drying brushes, then out at the garden beyond the window.

"He was fair," she said. "He was strong. And he never stopped listening. That's the kind of famous that matters."

The girl nodded slowly. And Boots smiled.

Mark might have left the ring, the dance floor, and the world behind, but in every canvas, she completed and every hand she played, his legacy unfolded again. Quietly. Honestly. Still in the middle.

The spaghetti always came out first. That was tradition. Frankie Jr. would ladle it out in big, steaming heaps onto everyone's plate while his daughter Mia recited grace in a voice just loud enough to command silence. On these nights, the family table transformed into something more sacred than Sunday Mass, because tonight, like every second Friday of the month, they told "Champ" stories.

It started simple. Frankie's son, little Joey, would ask, "Did Grandpa Conn really fight Rocky Marciano?" And Frankie Sr., still wearing his shop apron, flour dusted on his forearm, would chuckle and say, "No, no. He referred him, Joey. But he took more punches than you'd think just standing in the middle."

The laughter that followed was always warm, always reverent. Mark Conn was gone, but in this house, in this family, he was not forgotten. His name lived in the pauses between stories, the extra pinch of garlic in the sauce (Boots swore it was "just how Mark liked it"), the jazz records playing low in the background, even the bridge deck shuffled near the window seat.

Mia, now thirteen, had her own memory, small but vivid. "I remember his voice," she'd say with a far-off look, "telling me to keep my feet planted before I speak. That I'd sound stronger if I didn't rush." Her mother would nod, adding, "He told me that before job interviews, too."

The stories never came from a script. Sometimes they were about boxing. Like when he called the Ali-Bonavena match and came home with his shirt drenched in sweat, not his own. Other times, they were personal: the time he let Frankie skip school to watch him referee, or when Susan, his daughter, painted his portrait and he cried in private, not knowing how to say thank you.

A visitor walks past the images and old uniforms of the Flying Tigers at the Anti-Japanese War Museum in Dayi County in China's Sichuan province in 2005. Museums and memorials in China and the U.S. remember the AVG.

Joey loved the loud ones best. "Tell the one where he made the two fighters stop mid-round so the doctor could tie his shoe!" And Frankie would reenact the moment, pausing, raising a finger: "Time out!", and the kids would fall over laughing.

In a family filled with artists, jokers, and athletes, Mark Conn's presence wasn't just a ghost. It was a compass. His discipline passed to Mia's piano recital prep. His fairness shaped how Joey stood up for a friend at school. And his humor? That lived on in Frankie's impromptu kitchen toasts, often ending with, "Break, boys! Break!" as if they were all stepping out of an invisible ring.

The most worn photo in the house hung above the dining room hutch. It showed Mark mid-ring, arm extended between two fighters, face tight with calm command. But tucked beside it was the real treasure, a photo Boots took on a quiet Sunday: Mark in a cardigan, bridge cards in hand, with Joey asleep on his chest. No stage lights. No crowd. Just love.

As the grandchildren grew older, they asked better questions. "Was he scared in the war?" "Did he regret anything?" "Why didn't he ever write a book?" To which Frankie always said, "Your Grandpa didn't need a book. He wrote himself into every one of us."

One spring day, Joey came home from school with bruised knuckles and a note from the principal. He'd punched a kid who'd mocked Mia's speech impediment. Frankie wanted to be mad, but instead, he looked his son in the eye and asked, "Did you warn him first?"

Joey nodded. "Just like Champ said. I told him to break."

Frankie closed his eyes, smiled, and whispered, "That's my father's grandson."

And so, at that dinner table in a sunlit Florida kitchen, amid marinara stains and bridge hands, the next generation of Conn didn't just remember a referee, a father, a war hero. They remembered a man who stood for fairness, who taught grace through action, and who, in every whispered story, reminded them that legacies are not built in arenas, they're built in hearts.

In the quiet corridors of Madison Square Garden, where echoes of gloves on flesh and roars from balconies still lingered in the cement, a plaque was mounted beneath the old photograph wall. It did not feature a fighter. No title belts, no victory poses.

Just a man in black, arms stretched between titans, sweat soaking his collar, eyes locked in calm command. Below it, a simple line: "Mark Conn – The Man in the Middle."

The tribute wasn't loud, wasn't flashy, but it stopped visitors in their tracks. For decades, Conn had been the thread holding the fabric of boxing together when tempers flared and blood ran hot. And now, even in his absence, his legacy refused to sit still.

On the 10th anniversary of his passing, Madison Square Garden hosted a retrospective titled *Voices of the Ring: The Referees Who Shaped Boxing History*. And front and center stood Mark Conn.

The sports press had a field day. Columns filled with headlines that read like hymns.
"He Called Ali Clean."
"Controlled Foreman's Fury."
"Caught LaMotta's War Without Breaking a Sweat."

Writers dug into archives, revisiting his 219 officiated bouts like archaeologists uncovering hidden art. The footage, grainy yet electric, told a story words couldn't contain.

One clip showed Conn stepping between George Foreman and a staggering opponent, his hand firm on Foreman's chest, the other motioning the ringside doctor. Another showed him in the Ali vs. Bonavena fight, his voice ringing above the crowd: "Break! Back clean!" The fighters obeyed, as if the sound itself was sacred.

At the press conference launching the MSG tribute, former champion "Irish" Danny Quinn took the mic with misty eyes. "Some refs wanted to be seen," he said, voice low. "Mark just wanted the fight to be fair. And we trusted him with our lives. That ain't poetic, that's real."

The New York Times ran a Sunday feature titled: *The Third Man Who Made Every Match Better*. Inside was a black-and-white photo taken in 1950, LaMotta vs. Mitri. Conn stood in the storm, 15 rounds of fury swirling around him, and yet, his presence radiated stillness. Beneath it, the caption read:
"He never threw a punch. But every fight changed when he stepped in."

Boots attended the exhibit with Frankie and his kids. She wore her best business suit and red lipstick, Mark's favorites. As she moved through the halls, she touched each frame as if straightening a memory.

At the video booth, she lingered long on the clip of Mark raising Ali's hand. She whispered to herself, "He always said, 'The fight is never about you. Make it safe, make it fair, and then get out of the way.'"

Frankie, standing beside her, chuckled. "And then go home and teach piano, tell corny jokes, and fall asleep during the bridge."

The tribute ended with a looping recording of Conn's voice, captured from a 1972 interview. "I wasn't the best fighter. Wasn't the best pilot either. But in the ring, I knew how to read a man. I knew when to stop it. I knew how to protect them from each other, and from themselves. That's what a ref's job really is."

The voice faded. Visitors stayed silent. Some dabbed their eyes. Others just nodded.

As they left the exhibit, Joey asked his father, "Do you think people will remember me like that one day?"

Frankie smiled, wrapping an arm around his son. "If you live with honor like Grandpa did, they won't forget."

Mark Conn had no statue. No bronze fist in the air. But through stories, reels, and reverence, his legacy lived on, not because he demanded the spotlight, but because he always knew how to step into the chaos, whisper "Break," and let greatness happen around him.

The house was quieter now, as if the walls themselves were holding their breath. MJ sat at the old upright piano in the den, fingers resting lightly on the keys, not pressing, just touching. A faint sunbeam filtered in through the linen curtain, catching the dust that danced lazily in the still air. Boots had gone for her morning walk. Frankie had flown back to New York with his kids. And MJ had stayed behind, choosing silence over the noise of goodbye.

The piano still smelled faintly of lemon oil, like it had on that first day. Mark had been the one to sit beside her, guiding her small hands into chords, grinning when she fumbled, nodding seriously when she got it right. "Every good rhythm got a stumble in it," he'd said. "Same with life. Just keep time and keep going."

She played that now, his favorite old blues scale, simple, humble, warm. The notes fell like slow rain, gentle and forgiving.

Above the piano, taped to the wood, was an old photo, Mark in his referee blacks, arms outstretched between Ali and Bonavena. You could barely see his face, but the presence was unmistakable. Steady. Calm. Unmoved even in the hurricane of fists and fame.

MJ chuckled quietly. "You looked like a conductor up there," she whispered. "Except instead of violins, you had heavyweight explosions and egos twice your size."

But what stayed with her, even more than the fight stories or the bridge nights or the Toastmasters routines, was that last afternoon. Just a few days before he passed. She had flown down the moment Frankie called. Mark was frailer than she expected, thinner, paler, his voice raspier. But the eyes? Still sharp. Still with that glint of stubbornness that said, *not yet.*

He was sitting up in bed when she arrived, watching an old boxing match on mute.

"Which one?" she had asked.

"Me and Foreman. Well, not me and Foreman. I wasn't dumb enough to get in there with him," he rasped with a smirk.

MJ laughed. "You referred it, didn't you?"

"Damn right. Controlled that storm like a weatherman with a whistle."

She pulled up the wooden chair and held his hand, bony and spotted now, but still strong in its grip. "You ready to rest?" she had asked.

Mark gave a sideways grin. "Nah., I told Boots I'd give her another 20."

MJ frowned gently. "You're 92, Grandpa."

He winked. "Then I'd better get moving."

It wasn't denial. It was his humor. That quiet blade of resilience. He wasn't pretending to cheat death. He was just promising to greet it with a punchline.

They sat in silence a while. Then he'd asked, "Still playing?"

She nodded. "Every week."

"Good. Never stop."

Then he looked at her, eyes glistening. "Tell Frankie… I didn't mean to be hard on him."

"He knows," she said. "He always knew."

Mark closed his eyes. "Sometimes… a ref forgets he's also a father."

MJ blinked back tears at that. Not because of regret, but because of the clarity in it.

Later that evening, when she kissed his forehead and whispered goodnight, he opened his eyes one last time and said, "See you in another 20."

It had taken her a while to realize what he meant.

Not twenty minutes. Not twenty days.

Twenty years.

He meant the long game. The stories passed down. The quiet tributes. The bridges were built over time. That he would live again through memory, through laughter, through music and the ring, and every shout of "Break!" that echoed in the right moment.

Now, MJ played the final notes of the song. No flourish. Just the truth of a simple melody held together by love.

She stood up, placed her hand on the piano lid, and whispered, "You were the best conductor I ever had."

Then she turned off the light and let the silence hold him, his rhythm still alive in the wood, in the keys, in the space between each pause.

It sat in the center of the mantle, encased in glass that gleamed when the sun tilted just right through the Florida afternoon haze. A single red boxing glove. The leather cracked at the knuckles; the laces faded to a ghostly cream. A gold plaque at the bottom read:

Mark Conn
Referee, Fighter, Father, Friend
"Break!"

Visitors often paused in front of it. Some with reverence, some with curiosity. Most had no idea whether the glove belonged to LaMotta, Ali, or Foreman. But they always asked the same question.

"Did he fight?"

And the answer, invariably, came with a smile.

"He did," Frankie would say. "Just not always with fists."

The glove wasn't from any world title bout. It wasn't even a fighter's glove. It was Mark's. From his amateur days, long before the striped shirt, long before the Garden lights or the Flying Tigers. It had seen more training bags than noses. But it meant something because of what it survived. What he survived.

Boots had found it when clearing out the cedar chest after his passing. Beneath folded letters, Toastmasters trophies, yellowing clippings, and a crumpled-up program from LaMotta-Mitra. She held it to her chest for a long time before setting it aside. Later, she brought it to MJ and Frankie.

"We should display it," she said quietly. "Let people see what he carried."

Frankie had the case made. MJ printed the quote. And so, it became the centerpiece, not because of the glove itself, but because of the life it represented.

The house was quieter now, but not solemn. Boots still played bridge on Tuesdays. Frankie still cracked jokes too loudly. MJ still played piano every visit. And the grandkids, now teenagers, had taken to calling it *Champ House.* They never knew the full weight of what it meant, but they felt it.

That glove became a totem. A memory keeper. It stood for the thousand fights Mark had refereed, but also for the unseen ones: staying gentle in war, showing up as a father even when exhausted, making his kids laugh through grief, holding his wife's hand as she walked away, never raising his voice when life tested him, standing firm when the world said, *Give up.*

It stood for every time he chose fairness over fame. Grace over pride. Humor over bitterness.

During one family dinner, Frankie caught his son staring at the glove.

"You wanna wear it someday?" he asked, half-kidding.

The boy thought for a moment. "Not to fight. But… maybe to remember."

That was the legacy Mark left behind.

Not just a career of headlines or highlight reels. But a rhythm of presence. The sound of fairness shouted loud enough for the world to hear. The image of a man with arms stretched between titans, asking them to hold back for just a second.

To *break*.

To breathe.

To remember they were still human.

That glove, encased in its silent shrine, whispered all that. It said: *This man lived fully. He fought with purpose. He laughed with his whole chest. He loved without flinching. And he left the world better referred than he found it.*

MJ had once tried writing a song about it. But no melody felt big enough.

Boots painted it instead, deep reds and shadowed corners, the glove floating in space like a relic. She titled it simply: **"Still Fighting."**

At Mark's memorial, the glove sat beside the podium. Fighter after fighter, ref after ref, friend after friend passed by. Some saluted. Some kissed the glass. Some just touched it and smiled.

Ali's daughter had sent flowers. "Daddy respected very few men in the ring," she wrote. "Mark Conn was one of them."

Frankie read that aloud and looked toward the glove. "Told ya, Pop. You were the champ."

The room clapped, not for a fighter who won belts, but for a man who fought the kind of battles that never make the news.

Now, years later, that glove still catches the afternoon sun just so. And in the quiet flicker of light on its cracked leather surface, a story endures.

One of fairness. Fire. Family. And a final smile whispered through the years:

"See you in another 20."

A group of 52 U.S. World War II veterans who had served in China, including members of the Flying Tigers, visited Chongqing, China, in 2005 to attend memorial events.

Appendix

Mark Conn boxing record as Referee 222 bouts

From 1946-1986 (40 years)

Segment 1: Early Years of Refereeing (1946–1947)

Date	Winner	Result	Loser	Decision Type
1947-11-21	Billy Graham	W	Rocco Rossano	SD
1947-11-12	Herbie Kronowitz	W	Andres Gomez	UD
1947-10-21	Joe Lucas	D	George Wright	PTS
1947-10-21	Marcel Theriault	W	Roosevelt McKinney	KO
1947-10-21	Carl Taulman	W	Henry Gorman	PTS
1947-10-21	Pat Brady	W	Lenny Durham	PTS
1947-10-21	Mario Moreno	W	Frankie Dell	PTS
1947-09-18	Sonny Horne	W	Nick Kashuba	UD
1947-08-19	Vern Lester	W	Andres Gomez	TKO

Date	Winner	Result	Loser	Decision Type
1947-08-11	Lee Savold	W	Alberto Marchione	TKO
1947-06-16	Ruby Kessler	W	Patsy Spataro	TKO
1947-04-15	Henry Jordan	W	Norman Rubio	TKO
1947-02-08	Joey Fontana	W	Frankie Rubino	UD
1947-01-02	Tony LaBua	W	Justin Johnson	KO
1946-11-26	Harold Green	W	Joe Bennett	UD
1946-10-16	Norman Rubio	W	Tony DeRosa	UD
1946-10-01	George Kochan	W	Joe Reddick	UD
1946-08-20	Jimmy Hooper	W	Tony Gargiso	TKO
1946-06-17	Jim Neville	W	Harry Berntsen	TKO

Date	Winner	Result	Loser	Decision Type
1946-05-27	Steve Belloise	W	Coley Welch	TKO
1946-05-08	Billy Graham	W	Pedro Biesca	UD
1946-04-17	Joe Governale	W	Bobby Berger	UD

Segment 2: Post-War Boxing Scene (1947–1951)

Date	Winner	Result	Loser	Decision Type
1951-08-29	Kid Gavilan	W	Billy Graham	SD
1951-07-12	Rocky Marciano	W	Rex Layne	KO
1951-05-11	Walter Cartier	W	Gene Hairston	SD
1951-04-13	Bob Baker	W	Elkins Brothers	UD
1951-	Rex Layne	W	Bob Satterfield	TKO

Date	Winner	Result	Loser	Decision Type
03-09				
1951-01-26	Kid Gavilan	W	Paddy Young	MD
1950-12-29	Gene Hairston	W	JT Ross	KO
1950-12-08	Bob Murphy	W	Jimmy Beau	TKO
1950-11-10	Laurent Dauthuille	W	Paddy Young	UD
1950-10-20	Roland LaStarza	W	Duilio Spagnolo	UD
1950-09-27	Ezzard Charles	W	Joe Louis	UD
1950-08-24	Pat Marcune	W	Bill Bossio	SD
1950-08-07	Rocky Compitello	W	Freddie Lott	UD
1950-07-12	Jake LaMotta	W	Tiberio Mitri	UD

Date	Winner	Result	Loser	Decision Type
1950-06-22	Carmine Fiore	W	Al Costantino	TKO
1950-05-26	Kid Gavilan	W	Georgie Small	UD
1950-04-21	Johnny Saxton	W	Joe Miceli	SD
1950-03-10	Charley Fusari	W	Jimmy Flood	UD
1950-02-15	Jimmy Beau	W	Jose Basora	UD
1950-01-02	Jimmy Watkins Jr	W	Giuseppe Colasanti	UD
1949-12-01	George Kaplan	W	James P. Connolly	TKO
1949-11-17	George Kaplan	W	Johnny Bassett	TKO
1949-11-02	Walter Cartier	W	Gene Hairston	UD
1949-09-23	Jimmy Flood	W	Ernie Durando	KO

Date	Winner	Result	Loser	Decision Type
1949-08-08	Sandy Saddler	W	Johnny Rowe	TKO
1949-06-30	Jimmy Flood	W	Herbie Kronowitz	UD
1949-05-04	Jose Basora	W	Henry Brimm	MD
1949-02-10	Joey Carkido	D	Angelo Morganti	SD
1949-02-02	Paddy DeMarco	W	Humberto Sierra	UD
1949-02-02	Archie Devino	W	Filiberto Osario	TKO
1949-01-14	Vince Foster	W	Tony Pellone	KO
1948-12-06	Jimmy Warren	W	Johnny Wolgast	UD
1948-11-23	Joe Miceli	W	Al Pennino	UD
1948-11-12	Kid Gavilan	W	Tony Pellone	UD

Date	Winner	Result	Loser	Decision Type
1948-11-01	Paddy DeMarco	W	Bernie Bernard	UD
1948-10-21	Leo Milito	W	Nat Harden	UD
1948-09-23	Ike Williams	W	Jesse Flores	TKO

Segment 3: Golden Gloves & Rising Champions (1951–1955)

Date	Winner	Result	Loser	Decision Type
1955-05-27	Carmelo Costa	W	Lulu Perez	UD
1955-05-09	Isaac Logart	W	Ludwig Lightburn	UD
1955-04-29	Chico Vejar	W	Giampaolo Melis	TKO
1955-04-18	Gene Poirier	W	Johnny Busso	TKO

Date	Winner	Result	Loser	Decision Type
1955-04-04	Gil Turner	W	Gene Fullmer	UD
1955-03-21	Joe Rowan	W	Wayne Bethea	SD
1955-02-28	Pat Lowry	W	Pete Adams	UD
1955-02-17	Tommy Jackson	W	Leo Johnson	TKO
1955-02-04	Kid Gavilan	W	Ernie Durando	SD
1955-01-10	Bobby Bell	W	Rudy Garcia	UD
1955-01-03	Joe Klein	W	Gerald Dreyer	TKO
1954-12-20	Pete Adams	W	Jimmy Martinez	MD
1954-12-06	Italo Scortichini	W	Chico Varona	UD
1954-11-22	Oakland Billy Smith	W	Archie McBride	TKO

Date	Winner	Result	Loser	Decision Type
1954-11-01	Bobby Jones	W	Moses Ward	UD
1954-10-11	Bobby Dykes	W	Ted Olla	UD
1954-09-20	Hector Constance	W	Chico Varona	SD
1954-09-06	Jesse Turner	D	Ted Olla	SD
1954-08-16	Gerald Dreyer	W	El Conscripto	TKO
1954-08-02	Floyd Patterson	W	Tommy Harrison	TKO
1954-07-12	Floyd Patterson	W	Jacques R. Crecy	TKO
1954-06-26	Carmen Basilio	W	Al Andrews	UD
1954-06-07	Archie Moore	W	Bert Whitehurst	TKO
1954-05-24	Pedro Gonzales	W	Ralph Jones	SD

Date	Winner	Result	Loser	Decision Type
1954-05-10	Floyd Patterson	W	Jesse Turner	UD
1954-04-12	Eduardo Lausse	W	Jesse Turner	SD
1954-02-26	Libby Manzo	W	Pat Mallane	MD
1954-01-25	Tommy Jackson	W	Rex Layne	TKO
1953-12-28	George Benton	W	Bobby Jones	SD
1953-11-30	Freddie Herman	W	Brian Kelly	TKO
1953-11-09	James J. Parker	W	Edgardo Romero	UD
1953-10-12	Joe Klein	W	Rocky Casillo	MD
1953-09-21	Orlando Zulueta	W	Paddy DeMarco	SD
1953-08-24	Wallace "Bud" Smith	W	Charley Spicer	RTD

Date	Winner	Result	Loser	Decision Type
1953-07-07	Irvin Steen	W	Joe Miceli	UD
1953-06-09	Jimmy Herring	W	Sal DiMartino	UD
1953-05-19	Ralph Jones	W	Rocky Tomasello	UD
1953-03-16	Ralph Jones	D	Danny Womber	SD
1953-01-23	Willie Troy	W	Bobby Jones	SD
1952-12-29	Floyd Patterson	W	Lalu Sabotin	TKO
1952-12-08	Pierre Langlois	W	Harold Green	SD
1952-11-24	Ike Williams	W	Pat Manzi	TKO
1952-11-24	Chico Vejar	W	Sonny Luciano	TKO
1952-11-10	Walter Cartier	W	Otis Graham	TKO

Date	Winner	Result	Loser	Decision Type
1952-08-11	Eddie Compo	W	Teddy Davis	SD
1952-03-24	Phil Burton	W	Clarence Harbin	UD
1952-03-11	Billy Hazel	W	Raul Esqueda	MD
1952-02-11	Tony Pellone	W	Jackie O'Brien	SD
1951-11-16	Paddy DeMarco	W	Eddie Chavez	UD
1951-09-25	Johnny Williams	W	Jimmy DeCerio	TKO

Segment 4: Mid-Career Highlights (1955–1959)

Date	Winner	Result	Loser	Decision Type

Date	Winner	Result	Loser	Decision Type
1959-08	Alex Miteff	W	Alonzo Johnson	-
1959-06	Dick Tiger	D	Rory Calhoun	-
1959-05	Eddie Jordan	W	Bill Flamio	-
1959-03	Charley Scott	W	Isaac Logart	-
1959-02	Jose Torres	W	Eddie Wright	-
1959-01	Emile Griffith	W	Gaylord Barnes	-
1959-01	Stefan Redl	W	Danny Russo	-
1958-11	Victor Zalazar	W	Otis Woodard	-
1958-11	Candy McFarland	W	Isidro Martinez	-
1958-10	Isaac Logart	W	Rudell Stitch	-

Date	Winner	Result	Loser	Decision Type
1958-07	Gaspar Ortega	W	Mickey Crawford	-
1958-06	Tony DeCola	W	Peter Schmidt	-
1958-05	Johnny Busso	W	Lahouari Godih	-
1958-04	Stefan Redl	W	Charlie Cummings	-
1958-03	Garnet Hart	W	Duke Harris	-
1958-01	Jimmy Archer	W	Danny Russo	-
1957-12	Gale Kerwin	W	Jimmy Archer	-
1957-11	Gene Fullmer	W	Neal Rivers	-
1957-08	Gene Armstrong	W	Rudy Sawyer	-
1957-06	Gale Kerwin	W	Tony DiBiase	-

Date	Winner	Result	Loser	Decision Type
1957-05	Archie McBride	W	Willi Besmanoff	-
1957-03	Isaac Logart	W	Gil Turner	-
1957-03	Ike Chestnut	W	Gil Cadilli	-
1957-02	Isidro Martinez	W	Bobby Courchesne	-
1956-12	Gaspar Ortega	W	Tony DeMarco	-
1956-12	Italo Scortichini	W	Wilf Greaves	-
1956-11	Miguel Berrios	W	Flash Elorde	-
1956-09	Wayne Bethea	W	Joe Bygraves	-
1956-09	Harold Carter	W	Johnny Summerlin	-
1956-08	Joey Giambra	W	Rocky Castellani	-

Date	Winner	Result	Loser	Decision Type
1956-07	Tony Anthony	W	Tony Johnson	-
1956-06	Ludwig Lightburn	W	Jake Josato	-
1956-05	Gene Fullmer	W	Charles Humez	-
1956-05	Charley Cotton	W	Joey Giardello	-
1956-04	Rory Calhoun	W	Jackie LaBua	-
1956-03	Hardy Smallwood	W	Ray Drake	-
1956-02	Miguel Berrios	W	Bobby Bell	-
1956-02	Miguel Berrios	W	Bobby Courchesne	-
1956-01	Johnny Sullivan	W	Tony Johnson	-
1955-12	Yama Bahama	W	Giampaolo Melis	-

Date	Winner	Result	Loser	Decision Type
1955-12	Paolo Rosi	W	Lulu Perez	-
1955-11	Eduardo Lausse	W	Gene Fullmer	-
1955-11	Danny Giovanelli	W	Danny Jo Perez	-
1955-10	Ludwig Lightburn	W	Hoacine Khalfi	-
1955-10	Lulu Perez	W	Bobby Courchesne	-
1955-09	Jimmy Slade	W	Archie McBride	-
1955-08	Giampaolo Melis	W	Rinzy Nocero	-
1955-07	Tony Puleo	W	Libby Manzo	-
1955-06	Vince Martinez	W	Chico Varona	-
1955-06	Billy Collins	W	Vern Stevenson	-

Segment 5: Late Career & Final Bouts (1959–1986)

Date	Winner	Result	Loser	Decision Type
1986-11-14	Felipe Julio	D	Keith McKinney	SD
1983-10-14	Kenny Snow	W	Willie Preston	MD
1974-11-11	Jean Claude Bouttier	W	Garry Broughton	TKO
1974-08-19	Davey Vasquez	W	Andres Torres	MD
1974-07-15	Jose Fernandez	W	Sammy Goss	SD
1974-05-27	Eduardo Santiago	W	Livio Nolasco	MD
1973-10-29	Dario Hidalgo	W	Jose Rodriguez	SD
1973-10-08	Vito Antuofermo	W	Tony Kid Durango	UD
1972-	Esteban De	W	George Foster	TKO

Date	Winner	Result	Loser	Decision Type
04-10	Jesus			
1970-12-07	Muhammad Ali	W	Oscar Bonavena	TKO
1970-10-05	Ricardo Delgado	W	Davey Vasquez	MD
1970-02-16	George Foreman	W	Gregorio Peralta	UD
1969-10-31	Mike Quarry	W	Ruben Figueroa	SD
1969-10-31	Pedro Agosto	W	Bob Felstein	SD
1969-07-14	Donato Paduano	W	Billy Lonergan	TKO
1969-03-14	Chuck Wepner	W	Roberto Davila	MD
1968-11-15	Luis Rodriguez	W	Joe Shaw	UD
1968-09-11	Frank DePaula	W	Jimmy McDermott	TKO

Date	Winner	Result	Loser	Decision Type
1968-05-24	Bob Foster	W	Dick Tiger	KO
1968-05-10	Victor Melendez	W	Ulysses Jimenez	UD
1967-04-17	Nino Benvenuti	W	Emile Griffith	UD
1966-09-21	Joe Frazier	W	Oscar Bonavena	SD
1966-06-23	Buster Mathis	W	Everett Copeland	TKO
1965-08-25	Bobby Cassidy	W	Isaac Logart	TKO
1965-02-26	Zora Folley	W	Oscar Bonavena	UD
1964-11-13	Billy Stephan	W	Ski Goldstein	KO
1964-06-19	Johnny Persol	W	Bobo Olson	MD
1964-02-07	Joey Archer	W	Holly Mims	SD

Date	Winner	Result	Loser	Decision Type
1963-07-20	George Benton	W	Allen Thomas	UD
1963-02-16	Joey Archer	W	Blair Richardson	UD
1962-08-04	Wilbert McClure	W	Farid Salim	UD
1962-06-16	Carlos Hernandez	W	Paolo Rosi	TKO
1962-05-19	Muhammad Ali	W	Billy Daniels	TKO
1962-02-26	Ricky Ortiz	W	Frank Sallee	UD
1962-02-26	Billy Bello	W	Tito Velez	UD
1961-12-16	Dick Tiger	W	William Pickett	UD
1961-11-25	Yama Bahama	W	Farid Salim	MD
1961-10-30	Tony Hughes	W	Rodolfo Diaz	SD

Date	Winner	Result	Loser	Decision Type
1961-07-08	Jackie Donnelly	W	Paolo Rosi	MD
1961-05-20	Jorge Fernandez	W	Ted Wright	UD
1961-04-08	Jorge Fernandez	W	Denny Moyer	UD
1961-02-13	Paolo Rosi	W	Tommy Tibbs	UD
1960-12-17	Emile Griffith	W	Luis Rodriguez	SD
1960-10-31	Billy Hunter	W	Reiniero Rey Lopez	KO
1960-10-17	Jose Gonzalez	W	Ted Wright	SD
1960-07-12	Benny Kid Paret	W	Garnet Hart	KO
1960-05-23	Jose Gonzalez	D	Guy Sumlin	MD
1960-03-14	Jose Gonzalez	W	Antonio Marcilla	MD

Date	Winner	Result	Loser	Decision Type
1960-02-01	Lahouari Godih	W	Roger Harvey	UD
1959-11-09	Doug Jones	W	Juan Pomare	SD

Mark Conn lived an exciting and inspiring life. The events presented in this story are rooted in real historical records and facts. However, in the interest of storytelling, certain descriptions and narratives have been embellished to add color and life to the tale.

I offer my deepest gratitude and appreciation to my sister, **Leda Moscarella**, whose constant encouragement kept me focused and inspired throughout this journey.

A heartfelt thanks also goes to my dear friends, **Carla Mattia** and **Daniel Carson**, for their invaluable help and belief in this project.

Without their support, this story may never have been told.

MJ Schultz

www.ingramcontent.com/pod-product-compliance
Lightning Source LLC
Chambersburg PA
CBHW070803240726

48654CB00007B/192